PRIDE IN THE PAST— FAITH IN THE FUTURE

T0116877

PRIDE IN THE PAST— FAITH IN THE FUTURE

A History of The First 75 Years of The University Club of Winter Park, Florida

iUniverse, Inc.

New York Bloomington

Pride in the Past—Faith in the Future

Copyright © 2010 by the University Club of Winter Park, Florida

All rights reserved. No part of this book may be used or reproduced by any means, graphic, electronic, or mechanical, including photocopying, recording, taping or by any information storage retrieval system without the written permission of the publisher except in the case of brief quotations embodied in critical articles and reviews.

iUniverse books may be ordered through booksellers, Amazon.com, or by contacting

iUniverse
1663 Liberty Drive
Bloomington, IN 47403
www.iuniverse.com
1-800-Authors (1-800-288-4677)

For all other inquiries and correspondence:
University Club of Winter Park
841 Park Avenue North
Winter Park, FL 32789
407-644-6149
ucwpfl@earthlink.net
www.universityclubwinterpark.org

Because of the dynamic nature of the Internet, any Web addresses or links contained in this book may have changed since publication and may no longer be valid. The views expressed in this work are solely those of the author and do not necessarily reflect the views of the publisher, and the publisher hereby disclaims any responsibility for them.

ISBN: 978-1-4502-6646-8(pbk)
ISBN: 978-1-4502-6647-5(ebk)

Back cover pen and ink sketch by
George Stewart, January 1994
Photographs from Club archives
and by Paul Enchelmayer

Printed in the United States of America

iUniverse rev. date: 11/08/10

Contents

The History Book Committee

In observance of the 75th Anniversary of the University Club of Winter Park, it was decided that an update of the Club History Books, published in 1959 and 1994, would be produced by an *ad hoc* committee. The committee was a part of an overall 75th Anniversary Group coordinated by Past President Diane Sandquist (2001-2002).

The Committee met at various times between November 2009 and August 2010. The members of the Committee included Max Reed, Paul Enchelmayer, Bob Reed, Robert Wilkinson, Florence Bacas Snow, with Mary Keck serving as the Committee Chair. They were aided by staff member Rebecca Van Horn and Member Charles Kulmann.

As Samuel Johnson discovered in creating the first dictionary in 1755, the Committee found that "one enquiry often gave occasion to another—and that to search was not always to find and to find was not always to be informed." It was a wonderful task.

There is no single author of this book. It is the result of the written contributions of the committee members, based on Board minutes, research, and anecdotal reminiscences by Club Presidents Emeriti. The Committee apologizes for any errors of commission or omission.

This book is dedicated to and in honor of long-time Member Bob Wilkinson for his loyalty, dedication, and service to the Club.

Preface

The initial published history of the University Club of Winter Park was recorded in the book *The First Twenty-Five Years* (1959), which was later incorporated into another book, *Sixty Years in Review* (1994). Thus, the complete history of the Club from 1934 to 1994 was compiled in these two books. They are in the Club Library.

This *ad hoc* History Book Committee's task of writing this latest history was to preserve the past history, to research noteworthy material in the archives and files and Board minutes from 1994 to 2010, and to integrate new information into the format of *Sixty Years in Review*.

The plan was somewhat complicated and time-consuming because it was necessary to merge recent information in the appropriate sections of the previous book. Special editing was also required to ensure that the content would coincide in style with the older versions of the book. The result was this new book, *Pride in the Past – Faith in the Future*, which covers the seventy-five years of Club history.

Members of the History Book Committee had credentials and expertise. Max Reed was a book Managing Editor in New York for twenty-three years, while Bob Reed was a writer and a publisher for thirty years following twenty years with public television. Paul Enchelmayer is a photographer and a retired Systems Manager for the City of Orlando. Florence Bacas Snow, retired attorney who spent thirty years as a litigator in various Courts, is a recent Club member. Mary Keck is retired from the U.S. Foreign Service and a former Vice President of House and Grounds; she has held many other Club positions and has a vast knowledge of Club records and archives.

Bob Wilkinson (President 1980-1981) a retired Senior Scientist with the Canadian Department of Defense, served as Parliamentarian of the Club for twenty-four years. His knowledge of the Club and past events in Winter Park has been invaluable to the Executive Board and others through the years. Diane Sandquist (founding President of the Community Foundation of Central Florida and Club President 2001-2002) coordinated the many activities celebrating the 75th Anniversary Celebration.

This book consists of vignettes, anecdotes, sketches, stories, arcane information, snippets of trivia, and some lost myths. It is hoped that by turns, it may inform, amuse, seduce, and bewilder. It was a labor of research — and love — made possible by the generosity of an anonymous donor, and without the hard work and professional expertise of Max and Bob Reed, it would have been impossible to produce this book.

Please enjoy this history of a unique Club.

Mary Keck, Chair
History Book Committee

Diane Sandquist, President 2001-2002 and
Coordinator, 75th Anniversary Celebrations

History Book Committee:
    Mary Keck, Chair, History Book Committee
    Paul Enchelmayer, President 2010-2011
    Max Reed, President 2009-2010
    Bob Reed, President 2007-2008
    Bob Wilkinson, President 1980-1981
    Florence Bacas Snow, Esq., VP Intellectual Activities 2010-2011

PART I

CHAPTER 1

The First Three Years

The University Club of Winter Park began, not as the inspiration of a group of intellectual graybeards, but as a gleam in the eye of a 28-year-old man who wanted to protect his job. He was Carter Bradford, the executive secretary of the Chamber of Commerce of Winter Park in 1934 when he wrote *Lest We Forget*, a book of reminiscences collected by the Club to celebrate its twentieth anniversary.

> I deserve no altruistic credit for my part in the organization. My contribution was merely part of my Chamber of Commerce duties in promoting any worthy project for the betterment of Winter Park. I must admit that, as a newlywed whose wife was still in college, at a time when stockbrokers were selling apples on street corners, necessity fired my ambition for worthy projects. My employers must feel that I deserved to hold that plush $30-a-week job, payable partly in cash and partly in due bills of business men who paid their annual $15 Chamber of Commerce dues in dry cleaning, groceries, gasoline, hair cuts, or hardware.

And Bradford commented later, "As one of the charter members and organizers of the University Club, I now sit back at the ripe old age of 48, and recall that it was conceived by the Winter Park Chamber of Commerce and born in those memorable Depression days without a dollar in its pocket; in fact, few thought it would ever have a pocket."

The town of Winter Park was at that time a community of about 3,000 year-round residents, though the population increased during the winter by visitors from the north. Many among these temporary residents were retired college faculty members, clergymen, lawyers, doctors, and others of similar education and background. There were also many permanent residents who had similar interests.

A small committee of the Chamber seized upon Bradford's suggestion that a town group of university men might like to meet on a regular basis during the winter months, for discussion and fellowship. Among the most active on that committee were Dr. Kenyon L. Butterfield, a retired college president, and Hiram Powers, a local realtor and son of a famous sculptor. This committee interviewed many likely members and found enthusiasm for the idea.

Carter Bradford again:

> For the organization meeting, I sent invitations to everyone I thought might have graduated from a recognized college or fairly respectable reform school. If my memory is correct, thirty gentlemen responded, met in the Chamber rooms, and the University Club was born.
>
> During the first year, the Chamber of Commerce provided the meeting place and underwrote all expenses for stationery, postage, stenographic work and refreshments. As for refreshments, I squeezed so many oranges (they were free) that at times I longed to pour a full gallon down the throat of every member. Well-fortified with vitamin C, our young organization grew and grew.

The group that gathered on that March 24 in 1934 had been invited by means of a penny postcard to an organizational meeting at 8:00 p.m. at the Chamber of Commerce building (then located on the site of the present City Hall at the corner of Park and Lyman Avenues). The men attending were enthusiastic about the proposed organization and two meetings were subsequently held before the long summer hiatus.

Winter Park, Fla
March 20, 1934

Dear Friend:

You are cordially invited to attend an informal meeting of college graduates and faculty members of our winter colony for an "acquaintance meeting," to be held Saturday evening, March 24th at 8:00 P.M. in the Winter Park Chamber of Commerce Building. Please extend this invitation to any of your friends who might be interested.

Sincerely yours
Dr. K. L. Butterfield, Hiram Powers
Carter Bradford, College Committee
Chamber of Commerce

It was intended that the organization should function without the formal structure of bylaws, constitution, committees, etc. The official head of the group was to be designated "chairman" (not "president") and no other officers were specified at that time.

The new Chairman was Dr. George M. Whicher, described as being (in the words of William E. Stark, long-time Secretary and 1956-1957 President):

> ...handsome, scholarly, witty retired college professor, acting chairman during the first year of the Club and president during the second year.

In speaking of the desirability of the new organization, Dr. Whicher said: "It will benefit all of us to get together, out of the hearing of our wives, and tell each other how great we used to be."

The new Club held one meeting following the organizational one, then disbanded for the long hiatus until the next

5

winter season. It was not until December 20, 1934 that meetings resumed.

Winter Park was, at that time, a very different community from the one today. Its very name suggested that it was a refuge from cold northern weather. Some famous persons had established residence in the village, attracted by the beauty of the place and by the presence of Rollins College. The college had received broad publicity through the dynamism of the president, Hamilton Holt, who had attracted outstanding scholars and lecturers. These had in turn attracted other persons who wished to share in the cultural climate.

The town was a small place, with lovely lakes not yet obscured by houses and walls. Great trees arched over the streets. Most of the homes were of wood-frame construction, usually modest in size. There were three large hotels within the village and it was five miles distant from Orlando, which was itself just a small city. Rollins College was a natural beauty, and a salubrious climate attracted winter residents of taste and attainment. It proved an ideal setting for the new Club to flourish.

At the meeting on December 20, 1934 under the chairmanship of Whicher, committees were appointed to nominate temporary officers, draft a constitution, and plan a program for the next meeting, which was scheduled for January 19, 1935.

The constitution/charter that was drafted by this committee and adopted by the membership was amended many times and established some features that prevailed throughout the first twenty-five years. It is clear however that the original members did not foresee the growth of the Club. For instance, the Constitution Committee saw no reason for a conventional set of officers. Instead, they felt that one person, called a Factotum, could do all the organizational work. Dr. Whicher believed this plan was "absurd" and the usual president, secretary, and treasurer were created.

From the beginning, the programs kept to a high standard. The format was invariably a lecture, nearly always presented by a Club member, followed by a discussion period. The Club members drew on their own training and experiences for the topics. The membership was composed of men of extraordinary attainment, whether in science, education, or government service. The Club was sometimes referred to as "an intellectual spa."

At the annual meeting on March 2, 1935, Dr. Whicher, the temporary Chairman pending the adoption of a constitution, was elected the first President. His vision of the Club was acute as reflected in a series of articles that were printed in the *Winter Park Topics*, a newspaper of the time, at the beginning of his term.

> It is hoped that next season the membership may be largely increased, that the programs may be maintained at the same high level, and that the University Club may in due measure become a center of intellectual activity among the men of the community.

At the end of the first season there were sixty-one members. By the next year, 152 members were counted.

By the start of the third season (1936-1937), it was apparent that larger quarters had to be found. The "foster home" at the Chamber of Commerce was too small to accommodate the growing membership.

The biweekly meetings, which had begun with dinner at one or another of the town's restaurants and adjournment to the Chamber for the program, drew increasing attendance. During the third season, a room adjoining the kitchen of the Alabama Hotel was used, with the usual dinner preceding. This arrangement avoided the awkward interval between dinner at a restaurant and then reassembling the members at the Chamber for the meeting.

So it was that the primary concern of the new Club became the problem of finding a place where the members could meet frequently in more convenient quarters.

Suggestions were made that an arrangement might be worked out with the Morse Golf Course (known later as the

Country Club) for use of the clubhouse on its property. This building had been erected during the real estate boom of the 1920s but was little used by the late 1930s. A committee was named to investigate the feasibility of this idea and, by the end of the season, it was a real possibility. Estimates of rental and equipment costs were made and contributions were invited.

When the members separated for the summer, the prospects of having their own club room in that building seemed bright but dependent on gathering further funds. The committee, composed of Chairman Arthur Harris, Colonel Wilgus, and Hiram Powers, was in charge of the project. In the fall the members found that the University Club plan had been blocked by the organization of a country club that had leased the clubhouse and was planning the development of a golf course.

However, a member returning from the north might have been puzzled by the sight of a new wing that had sprouted from that old clubhouse. That, the members learned, was the new home of the University Club.

Member Arthur Harris was the "angel," having kept the matter a close secret even from other members of the committee. And when the apparent conflict between the Club plan and the development of a golf course became known, Harris got approval for developing use of the clubhouse by both organizations. The plan involved adding a new wing for small gatherings of the University Club, as well as adding kitchen equipment and movable furniture, thus enabling the old part of the building to be available to the Club for dinners and meetings.

At the opening meeting of the season, held in the new Clubroom on December 4, 1937, the full extent of Arthur Harris's generosity was learned. All bills for building and equipment, amounting to more than $6,000, had been paid by Harris, who offered to turn the property over to the University Club with the obligation to pay only $2,000, in addition to the few hundred dollars raised previously. This debt would be discharged by ten annual payments of $200 with no interest.

The Club voted to accept this generous offer and began calling the structure the Little Harris Clubhouse. In a show of appreciation, Harris was elected President for 1939-1940.

University Club, Members 1934

CHAPTER 2

The Little Harris Clubhouse

T he nearly eleven years in the Little Harris Clubhouse, from December 1937 to April 1948, were marked by such rapid growth that the new quarters became a tight fit and were almost ludicrously inadequate. Nevertheless, habits were developed and purposes clarified that continued to give direction and system to the organization.

In the beginning there was no clear, generally understood idea of how the Clubhouse could be used to best advantage. This new Club could not be modeled on other university clubs but had to be developed by experience and adapted to the building and equipment and to the peculiarity of the membership.

During the first season, the new clubroom was open every afternoon but was rarely used except by a small group of bridge devotees. But the regular biweekly meetings with dinners, business affairs, and addresses became a habit. The large room in the Country Club building, connected to the clubroom by a narrow passage, was used for dinners and large evening meetings.

But the attractive clubroom with its comfortable armchairs and pleasant atmosphere did not lure members for sociability as had been expected. It seemed that the members did not feel the need for that kind of facility. Early in the next season, the Club began to learn what was wanted.

The type of activity, which began to be a distinctive feature of the organization, was the so-called Powwow, a word borrowed from the Algonquin language of the Native Americans and meaning a conference or meeting. This feature began almost by accident.

In the fall of 1938, after a six-month hiatus, an informal afternoon gathering opened the clubroom for the season. The members chatted so enthusiastically that it occurred to Fred Bartlett, Chairman of the House Committee, that the Club should have a weekly afternoon meeting. This experiment was tried with the hesitant approval of the members, and before the end of that season (1938-1939) two Powwows were needed to take care of volunteer speakers, on Tuesday and Friday afternoons. (The Tuesday meeting was discontinued in the early 1980s.)

The sixty-minute limit on the length of meetings, which became a tradition, began in the first year or two. Its most vigorous champions, the bridge players, now rushed to the tables in the rear of the meeting room on the stroke of four o'clock. At the Annual Meeting of the Club on March 9, 1940, one of the leaders of these affairs said of them:

> For those of you who have not yet formed the Pow-wow habit, it may be well to explain that in its present state of evolution, it is a sort of seminar on the whole range of human knowledge and curiosity. From another point of view, it is a laboratory in which men expose to the observer the heterogeneous contents of their minds. Incidentally, it is a practice ground for exercising one's ability in the use of speech as a means of conveying thought.
>
> Some of the topics have been chosen because of their general interest and we have sought speakers who were supposed to know something about them. ... In other cases we have left it to the speaker to choose the subject in which he could show himself to best advantage. ...
>
> Although we have discussed politics, economics, and religion, and have had vigorous debates, I think we have avoided undue heat or intolerance and, while nobody was convinced of the error of his ways, we have often got a better understanding of the other side.

At first, the subjects and speakers were agreed on by those who attended, the leg work being done by volunteer leaders, but in 1940 a Program Committee was put in charge of all meetings. The committee sought the help of members by questionnaires, and at the end of each season printed an annual program. The Little Harris Clubhouse was well adapted to such meetings.

The gatherings had a remarkable effect on the members' feeling for the Club. They had been proud to belong to a group that included such able men, and had listened with enjoyment and profit to the addresses given on alternate Saturday evenings, but with the Powwows the members began really to know each other, as members displayed their talents in debate or recounted personal experiences. Repeated contact with the same individuals made for familiarity and acquaintance growing into genuine friendship.

They not only made new friendships but revived old ones, sometimes encountering men with whom they had been in contact in previous years. There were also men whose important work had made them nationally known, such as Dr. Charles W. Stiles, director of the famous attack on hookworm infestation in the southern states, and Ray Stannard Baker who had come to be admired through his writing. "It was thrilling to know them and to find them friendly and unassuming," said former Secretary and Historian William Stark (President 1956-1957).

As the membership grew, the magnitude of the combined experience and knowledge of the members became impressive and suggested the quip that has been used ever since to control the pride of prospective speakers. "Whatever the subject and no matter how much you know about it, there will be one or more in the audience who can add to your knowledge."

Throughout the Little Harris Clubhouse era (1937-1948), the position of Powwow leader was one of importance and hard work. The two leaders were members of the Program Committee and shared with the Chairman the responsibility for arranging programs and securing speakers in accordance with general plans adopted by the committee. This division of labor made the Chairman's position less onerous than it became in later years and permitted him to give attention to programs for the regular evening meetings.

Many leaders contributed much to the success of the Club during its formative years. William Stark mentioned a few of them.

> Fred A. Hall, a social worker for many years with the Russell Sage Foundation, gave form to a number of club practices that still persist. His fine baritone voice was largely responsible for the success of a club quartet, which flourished for one or two seasons. As secretary of the Interracial Conference, he was a tireless worker for better race relations.

Orlo J. Price, Hall's partner during the years 1940-1942, a minister and prominent church official, was a man of fine mind with superior command of language.

David Robinson served continuously for three years. He was a popular member and expert bridge player, and an interesting conversationalist. For several years he was Chairman of one of the Winter Park civic commissions.

John Rogers, a plant pathologist, long connected with the U.S. Department of Agriculture, could always be relied upon to throw interesting light on topics related to science and, to the end of his life, he was a useful member of the Book Review Group.

During the eleven years in the Little Harris Clubhouse, the Club faced problems caused by its amazing popularity. Members became enthusiastic salesmen, writing to friends in their hometowns telling them about the wonderful Club. This had the effect of encouraging frequent proposals for enlargement of the Club quarters or moving to a new location.

The Little Harris Clubroom seated about seventy persons comfortably, but by the end of the 1938 season, 175 members were enrolled. In its last season at that location (1947-1948), the total had risen to 472 and the resulting compression can be imagined.

Attempts to get more room had begun when the clubroom had been in use little more than a year. On March 11, 1939, the House Committee was authorized to look up the cost of its proposal to extend the porch on the Webster Avenue side of the building. Four weeks later, it was decided to proceed with the addition to the present room if and when $1,000 had been subscribed. The condition was not fulfilled and the space shortage continued.

All chairs would be filled long before the scheduled time for a meeting, with standees in the corners, on the porch, and even outside the windows, to hear the speakers. If the facility was inadequate, it did not dampen the enthusiasm of the members for the cultural environment of the Club afternoons.

Interest was keen in the speakers, subjects, or both. Some of the lecture titles were "Entomology for the Layman" by Dr. Herbert Osborn and "Geology of Florida" by Dr. James H. Stoller. Both of these men, experts in their fields, were able to hold the interest of nonprofessional audiences.

"Germany in the 1880s and 1890s" was offered by eight or ten men who had studied there during that period, when a Ph.D. from a German university was considered essential evidence of top scholarship.

"A Saga of the Organ Pumper" by Charles L. Zorbaugh provoked general laughter from the surprising number of members who claimed to have pumped the bellows of church organs before electricity supplied the energy.

"A Visit to Bulgaria," a talk by William D. Street, was the story of the capture of a missionary — a Miss Stone — by bandits, and her release on payment of ransom by an emissary of President Woodrow Wilson. When the subject was opened for discussion, Member Ray Stannard Baker modestly admitted that he was the emissary.

War conditions and events necessarily affected University Club affairs in the late '30s and early '40s. Establishment of military bases in the vicinity brought a population change. Younger members were called into service, and colonels and generals were added to the membership. Rationing of food and fuel limited the menu and the amount of travel.

William Stark, Secretary during that time, wrote,

> On the whole, the mildly rigorous regimen was good for morale. We learned to walk, we revived our mastery of the bicycle. We moved our own furniture at dinner meetings, and served as busboys when the caterer's staff failed to appear. The strict limitation of building materials, mounting prices, and the cost-plus hedge of cautious contractors kept an exasperating brake on our repeated efforts to get more room.

In 1937, while the Club sought a meeting place of its own, it had voted to incorporate the Club. A lawyer member helped to formulate a charter defining the purpose of the organization, conditions of membership, responsibility of officers, adoption and amendment of charter and bylaws, and limitation of property and amount of indebtedness. The suggested charter was approved at the meeting of April 10, 1937, and seven members, all current or former officers, were named as incorporators. Three days later, the Judge of the Circuit Court gave his approval.

Members assumed that the transaction was complete and for four years lived in blissful ignorance of the fact that, as a club, it had no legal standing. A new member, Judge Frederick M. Peasley, a Connecticut lawyer with a habit of meticulous exactness, supplied an unexpected shock treatment. "The University Club has no members at all," he said, "because the incorporators never completed their responsibility for adopting bylaws defining membership." Four of the original seven immediately took the necessary action. An amended Charter was approved by the Circuit Court Judge in 1941, the new Bylaws adopted (see Appendix A), and the members of the voluntary association were made *bona fide* members of the corporation.

Since then the Charter has been amended from time to time, chiefly by broadening the base of membership and by increasing the permissible limits of indebtedness and value of the property. The Bylaws have undergone more frequent amendments.

The original invitation to join was issued to "college and university men" and the organization was properly named the University Club, but members soon began to urge admission of individuals who would add strength to the Club but held no collegiate degrees. For more than ten years, there were occasional verbal battles between those who thought that a university club should be rigid in upholding an academic background as a condition of membership and those who favored enough flexibility to admit some men whose education had been gained outside institutions of learning.

At that time, ten percent of the members could be nonde-greed men and some outstanding residents of Winter Park were elected, but when the quota was filled, members contin-ued to urge admission of friends or acquaintances. The pres-sure on the Membership Committee became so intense that, for several years, its makeup was kept secret.

For a time, the impatience of candidates and their sponsors for admission as "ten-per-centers" was countered by creating the classification of "seasonal guest," which involved pay-ment of the regular dues and renewal of application for each season.

Dissatisfaction continued and the next step was the intro-duction of the status of "associate," with all the privileges ex-cept the right to vote and hold office. Since associates paid regular dues, some members felt this injustice was "taxation without representation." Veteran Member Arthur B. Siebold led the attack and was supported by a postcard poll of mem-bers.

In January 1947, a plan was adopted that permitted the Membership Committee to recommend, in any one year, one nondegreed applicant for every four degreed men.

Some time later, the requirements for nondegreed appli-cants were changed to the current plan, in which in any given month, twenty percent of the number of members admitted over the previous twelve-month period are eligible for ad-mission. Two letters of recommendation from members and a three-quarters vote of the Membership Committee are also required. It is noted, however, that when a nondegreed mem-ber is elected, there are no limitations—voting, office-holding, committee participation, and the like—on that membership and many of them have been among the Club's most valuable officers and members.

The Club prospered in the Little Harris Clubhouse, with enthusiastic retired men crowding the premises. It was a glo-rious time.

CHAPTER 3

The Search for Space

The need for more room for the Club became more acute in those early days.

The problem of cost was ever present and was the chief reason for schemes to enlarge the Little Harris Clubhouse instead of moving to another location. Conflicting ideas among strong partisans for each of several proposals prevented a consensus in favor of any one of them. It is now clear that it was fortunate that this was so, because it prevented acceptance of proposals that might have resulted in possession of property far less satisfactory than the present building.

A committee was appointed in December of 1941 to study the problem of a permanent home. It recommended purchase of the lot at the Interlachen and Welbourne intersection with a frame building on it known as the Greenwood Apartments. An estimate was made of the cost of remodeling the structure for use as a clubhouse, and the committee was authorized to raise subscriptions up to $7,500.

A frequent feature of Club history has been generous offers by individual members. To avoid loss of the opportunity to secure this site while the committee sought subscriptions and members were discussing the proposal, a relatively new member, General Charles McC. Reeve, purchased the property and offered to sell it to the Club without profit to himself and on very easy terms of payment. General Reeve was an outstanding member, joining the Club at age 93 and remaining an active member until his death just weeks before his 100th birthday.

But a considerable difference of opinion arose as to the suitability of the property, and other locations were suggested. Dr. George Opdyke (Chairman of the Building Committee) contributed, at his own expense, an architect's drawing of a building that, to many, seemed too magnificent and too costly to be practicable. (The present Clubhouse was designed by the same architect, James Gamble Rogers, and looks much like that drawing.)

Discussions about the future were undertaken as the country entered World War II. At the Annual Meeting of March 7, 1942, General Reeve's offer was rejected. However, it was decided to have plans drawn for an enlargement of the Little Harris Clubhouse and to find out whether a lease of the ground for perhaps twenty years could be obtained from the City of Winter Park. A careful study of the scheme was ordered by the Executive Committee.

At a special meeting of the Club on March 18, 1942, Dr. Opdyke presented plans for an enlargement prepared by the architect Gamble Rogers, but the possibility of a ten-year lease was all that could be reported. The Executive Committee offered the following statement, which was approved almost unanimously.

1. No considerable enlargement of our building should be made until a satisfactory lease covering a considerable period is obtained.
2. While it appears that an enlargement and rearrangement of our clubhouse could be made with the consent of the Country Club, such a project should not be adopted hurriedly but must be studied carefully with a view to determining its adequacy for permanent use.
3. It is by no means certain that permanent location of the University Club on the restricted area available would be to the advantage of our Club. It is probable that a few years hence the future needs of the Club can be more clearly perceived.

4. The present moment is one of uncertainty. In the opinion of many, it is not a time for unnecessary expansion. We have been happy in our little clubhouse; we can continue to be happy in it during the war even if we are crowded.

In view of the above, the members of the Executive Committee were unanimous in recommending that plans for the enlargement of the Clubhouse should be postponed indefinitely, to be resumed at a later time when the question of tenure had been definitely answered, when obligations imposed by the war had been met, and when the future needs of the Club could be more clearly foreseen.

Following this, there was relative quiet regarding the space problem. Then, on March 25, 1944, a Committee on Future Accommodations was appointed to look for available sites and obtain estimates of costs for a new building compared to enlargement of the existing Little Harris Clubhouse.

At a meeting on February 17, 1945 the committee reported that the Country Club did not approve the plan to extend the Clubhouse, removing one of the chief causes of the disagreements. The members promptly voted to proceed with a campaign to secure a site and raise funds for a new building. A Financial Committee chaired by John Gowdy along with a Building Committee with William G. Atwood as Chair were appointed.

On March 26 the Building Committee suggested four possible sites with the size and price of each:

1. Corner Webster Avenue and Golfview Terrace
2. Osceola Avenue north of Osceola Court
3. Corner Webster Avenue and North Park Avenue
4. Corner New England Avenue and Alexander Place

The Committee recommended site 3, the largest of the four and the least expensive. After a lively discussion, during which the central location of site 4 was urged, the committee's choice was approved by a vote of 67 to 43.

A vote of thanks was tendered to Miss Jeannette Genius for her generous offer to reduce the price of the selected site from the listed figure of $9,000 to $5,000 and to contribute $1,000 to the Building Fund. (Miss Genius later became the wife of Hugh McKean. He served as President of Rollins College and was a long-time member of the Club.)

The question of location appeared to be settled and, during the next year, the Building Committee and the Finance Committee made progress. Floor plans were submitted for criticism by the members. Bertram Scott, who had relieved Bishop Gowdy as Chair of the Finance Committee, reported nearly $45,000 in subscriptions, pledges, and the sale value of the Little Harris Clubhouse. Then came a sudden shock.

At the Annual Meeting of March 8, 1947, the Building Committee presented a carefully prepared report explaining that some members were dissatisfied with the Park Avenue/Webster site. They wanted a more central location calling the site "too far out in the country," and had apparently convinced most of the members of the committee to join them. The committee now recommended that the Club sell the Park Avenue/Webster lots and purchase another site on Interlachen and New England Avenues. John Martin's residence on Genius Drive was also considered.

The committee's report surprised many of the members, but at an informal meeting called to discuss the proposals, it was evident that the "central location party" had done some active electioneering. A show of hands at the end of the meeting gave thirty-six in favor of the Martin house, seventeen for the Park Avenue lots already owned, and seventy for the Interlachen-New England site. It was explained that this was merely an expression of those present, and that a decision of the question must be deferred to a regular meeting. Nevertheless, the downtown boys went home elated and the rest dumbfounded.

The regular meeting of April 5, 1947 was remembered as one of the most exciting in the Club's history. The offer of the Martin house having been withdrawn, there were two opposing groups, each with devoted adherents. The atmosphere was tense, but the meticulous impartiality of Eugene Smith (President 1946-1947) kept the discussion orderly. Spokesmen for the Building Committee's latest recommendation stressed the importance of a central location near Rollins College and the exceptional opportunity to get one at a reasonable price.

A minority report by a member of the Building Committee urged retention of the Club's land on Park Avenue because 1) it would permit parking for more cars, 2) it was twenty-five percent larger than the proposed area, 3) it was rectangular in shape and bounded by three streets, making entrance and egress easy, and 4) it was adjacent to the open ground of the Morse Park/Country Club and the golf course.

After considerable lively discussion and presentation of differing views, the motion to adopt the Building Committee's recommendation was defeated, 62 to 51. When the tally was announced, the chairman of the Building Committee immediately moved that the committee be authorized to have detailed plans and specifications prepared for bids for the Park Avenue/Webster site. The motion passed unanimously.

The following year was a time of intense activity. The Finance Committee continued to build up the total of subscriptions and pledges. Then suddenly came a call for a special meeting, on December 5, 1947, to consider an unexpectedly favorable bid that would be withdrawn unless it was acted upon at once.

The minutes indicate that "about 150 were present in the Little Harris clubroom or the immediate vicinity." The Building Committee reported the lowest bid: $54,736 for the complete job for the new building as specified, with a reduction of $1,100 if asbestos roofing was substituted for tile, and $1,000 more if plaster on interior walls was omitted. The committee advised adoption of both these savings.

Temporary omission of one wing would have reduced the cost by another $10,000, but would have thrown the plan out of balance and required rearrangement of floor space. It was explained that necessary items not included in the bids might bring the cost up to about $60,000, which was $15,000 more than the amount available in cash and pledges.

Some conservatives urged caution because the Club might be biting off too big a mouthful. But the prevailing sentiment was enthusiastic endorsement of the whole program. The committee's recommendations for savings were rejected, and the complete bid was accepted by a vote of 67 to 38.

Three days later a joyful ceremony occured at the building site when the Mayor of Winter Park, along with the President of the Club (Russell P. Jameson, 1947-1948) and Colonel Atwood, Chairman of the Building Committee, spoke briefly. The long-hoped-for Clubhouse was actually started. The Club committed to a big enterprise, and a period of the finest kind of cooperative effort began.

Ground Breaking 1947

In reminiscences titled *Lest We Forget...Twentieth Anniversary*, William Stark (President 1956-1957) wrote

> Monday morning, December 8, 1947, marked a high point in the history of the University Club. At eleven o'clock, some fifty people had gathered on the Clubhouse site, several armed with cameras, which kept clicking as their owners flitted about the stage. Rudy

Matthews' open car, drawn up at one side served as a rostrum and orange trees laden with fruit furnished a colorful background.

President Jameson presided, introducing speakers and knights of the shovel with his customary grace. Speeches by Mayor Coleman, President Holt, and Colonel Atwood, were short but of high quality and happy portent. The Secretary, called upon for a bit of history, told a pathetic story of a fast-growing boy who for years had been pleading for long pants. At the end, the constricted frown breaks into a broad grin. The pants have been ordered.

Then the real work started. Six past presidents stepped forward in order of seniority and, with a few choice words and a determined grip on a super deluxe spade, loaned by Rollins College, sliced through the sod and removed a portion of soil with surprising deftness and no casualties. President Jameson (1947-1948) took the last bite and pronounced the ground broken.

Dr. Shippen (President 1936-1937), who habitually thought in meter, prefaced his spadework with a rhyme that will serve as a closing feature of this report.

'Tis far from *infra dig*, I ween
To take this spade in hand, Sir;
Nay, highly honored I have been,
The first to dig the sand, Sir.
Now "prosit" be our wineless toast!
Success to our endeavor!
Full soon a clubhouse may we boast,
Dear clubmates, comrades ever!

William Washburne, an engineer who succeeded Colonel Atwood as Chair of the Building Committee, kept a close watch as the structure was being erected. Clarence Coddington took charge of landscaping the grounds, including lawns, driveways, and parking areas, and gave a gift of azaleas to form a nursery of shrubs for future use.

A gift of tall palms from Miss Genius contributed to an attractive setting for the splendid building. Sale of the Little

Harris Clubhouse to the Country Club was arranged, with the right to defer moving until the new building was in condition to receive the Club's belongings. New equipment was ordered with date of installation or delivery similarly delayed.

The Finance Committee finished its drive for subscriptions before the annual exodus for the summer. The Treasurer's records show that 400 members contributed a total of $60,817. That amount is a record to be proud of as the total membership in January 1948 was 472, involving in some cases a high degree of self-sacrifice.

It had been hoped, in earlier plans for a new clubhouse, that incurring a debt could be avoided; or if that became impracticable, the charter limit of $10,000 would not be exceeded. However, it became clear by January that, for a time at least, that limit should be increased. Accordingly, the Charter was amended to increase the debt limit to $20,000 and the value of the real estate to $100,000.

A mortgage of $15,000 at four percent interest payable in installments over a period of fifteen years was generously offered by a member, R. T. Miller, Jr. Officers were authorized to borrow up to $5,000 on short-term notes to meet obligations pending collections of pledges.

The Board had tried to anticipate any difficulties, but when most of the members departed for the summer, the building was far from complete and would need constant supervision.

Further, the newly planted lawn required expert care. The latter need was provided by the landscape contractor, the former by appointing member Ihna T. Frary to represent the Building Committee. His skillful service throughout the summer, which included authorizing payments when due, settling unexpected questions, and so ensuring completion of the building on time, was exemplary.

Arriving at the point of actually moving into the new Clubhouse was not without problems. Frary, who had been designated to oversee the final phases of building and decorating the Club during the spring and summer of 1948, wrote the following in 1954.

The walls of the new clubhouse were up, the floor joists were being nailed in place when I was asked to take over the job of superintendence. As I had just designed and built my own house, some assumed, optimistically, that I knew something about the builder's trade.

The roofing tiles failed to show up when the roofers were ready for them, but with a covering of heavy building paper, it was deemed safe to lay the flooring. As this work progressed, I discovered one morning that seven-eighth-inch thresholds were being placed in the doorways. These would surely offer fine stumbling blocks—it was too late to throw them all out, but the one in the kitchen was planed down and a few eradicated.

Then one bright morning a truck-load of roofing tile showed up, and in a few days the roof was covered—the hottest red roof ever seen. Time and humidity have mellowed this color, so it is now quite good in tone.

The walls in the main room were to be tinted a soft green by mixing pigment with the plaster. This was a means of saving expense but when the time came to do this, the contractor assured us that only yellow would resist the action of lime on pigment. So the walls were given a creamy tint instead of green. Not to be fooled entirely on the use of green, that color was used on the walls of the coat room.

I made the wise suggestion that it might be well on occasion to curtain off the platform as a stage. To accomplish this, three sturdy hooks could be inserted in the roof timbers and a heavy wire stretched between them to carry a curtain.

For some reason this simple expedient raised a storm of protest. But, when the storm subsided, I quietly had the hooks screwed in place and painted white. Today they are covered with acoustic plaster, but Clarence Day assures me that their location was carefully marked for the benefit of future generations of less serious-minded members.

Frary, who commented that he had had more than twenty-five years experience as an interior decorator, was further disappointed that his suggested frieze to be applied under the eaves on the outside of the building was voted down. But he was pleased that many of his suggestions for accessories in the building were provided by various members, notably a reading-desk for the auditorium platform.

This desk had been designed for the space, and it so pleased Member Hamilton Gibson that he paid for it and suggested that there should be a pair of chairs to go with it on the platform.

Frary found a pair of antique Spanish arm chairs, which Gibson paid for and had repaired and reupholstered. Later, Gibson had shipped from New England two "Dartmouth" chairs (reproductions of a chair having associations with Daniel Webster) and a small book table. In February 1949, the President of the Club reported that the chairs for the auditorium platform, presented by Mr. Hamilton Gibson, are composed "by selecting the finest elements which have emerged in the evolution of furniture and combining them in one perfect symphony." (Later, the donation of the Japanese Gong was added to the platform; see Chapter 14.)

The Japanese Gong and Spanish Chairs

But Gibson wasn't through. On another occasion, wrote Frary, "He brought a rug from his home to the clubhouse, saying that it might fit the lobby floor…" I gave one look and said, "It will not go in the lobby, but it is exactly right for the rostrum and is far better than the Club could afford for that place."

When the House Committee asked him to secure estimates on draperies and a few other items, Member George Opdyke looked "lovingly" at the sample for the card room windows and said, "I'll pay for those curtains." He did the same for the small Library curtains. Suggestions for patterned draperies for the Auditorium, however, were summarily rejected with the comment that the male members did not want their meeting room "to look like a young lady's boudoir."

While some of the decorating was still going on and would continue for a few months, the new building was ready to receive the furnishings from the Little Harris Clubhouse. The time was May of 1948, the season was over, and the many Club members whose homes were elsewhere had left Winter Park.

Clarence M. Day, President of the Club in 1950-1952 later wrote

> The diary entry I made on May 25, 1948 reads as follows: "Spent all morning at the University Club with Al Dorn closing it up for good." Al had been custodian of the Club for several years. As I recall, we took down the outside awnings and then removed all the books from the shelves and wrapped each in newspaper and placed them in cartons, as was a yearly custom for prevention from mildew.
>
> The next date I have is August 8, 1948: "I moved some things from the old clubhouse to the new." This means that I packed my car full of coat hangers, songbooks, umbrella jars, cuspidors, ashtrays, unclaimed hats, etc., and took them over to the new building. Two days later my entry reads: "At University Club all day. I moved all the books this a.m. In the afternoon I had the Winter Park Moving Company finish carrying over

all the remaining items." As I recall it, the total expense was $22.

The moving of the physical items was a necessary chore, but as Day noted, "...had we not transferred the wonderful spirit of the University Club as it existed in the Little Harris Clubhouse up the street to these new and larger quarters, all would have been for naught."

When it was time for the absent members to return, everything was ready inside and out. As Frary wrote, "We had a good time worrying while it lasted. We did a pretty satisfactory job of building. We oldsters have gone down into our pockets pretty deep; now it's up to a new generation of members to carry on."

Park Avenue Entrance

Finally, the new Clubhouse was ready to receive the members. The old Clubhouse had become painfully inadequate, but affection for it and the good times there were bound to make it missed.

On the evening of November 6, 1948, members, together with their wives who had been invited for the occasion, had their first inside view of the new building. It was called "Wonderful!" "Perfect!" "What a change!" And others, marveling, said, "Look at the library. Can we ever fill all those shelves?" "Is the auditorium too big for our needs?" The membership stood at 507.

CHAPTER 4

The New Clubhouse

Life in the new Clubhouse brought many changes, and the adjustments, while not really painful, were frequently difficult. The membership, which had grown almost explosively in the first six or seven years, grew much more slowly, though there was rarely a regular meeting without the election of new members.

The greater space available in the new building made possible the extension of Club activities—among them development of a small Library and organization of interest groups among the members. This group activity added much to the value of Club membership. It provided an opportunity for close acquaintanceship and for exchange of ideas and experiences not possible in larger meetings in the auditorium.

In the Little Harris Clubhouse, only a dedicated bridge group had met on a regular basis. But during the first year in the new building in 1948, two new groups were formed. One was a Round Table, which soon became the Book Review Group. The other was the Camera Group. And a Duplicate Bridge Group was formed in the mid-1950s.

The first twenty-five years of the Club's existence also saw many changes in the city of Winter Park. It evolved from a place designed as a winter vacation spot and a retirement haven. The three large resort hotels, open only in the winter months, were open year round. The Little Harris Clubhouse had always closed from the end of April to the middle of October. After the first season in the new building in 1948, however, the practice of stopping all Club activity for nearly half the year seemed unreasonable.

A few years previously, the popularity of the Powwows had made it feasible to hold semiweekly sessions, in addition to the biweekly dinners during the season. With the new building and with the increase of permanent residents among the members, it was decided to hold a weekly Powwow through the entire summer, resuming the full schedule in the fall.

The Powwows had been, from their beginning in the early years of the Little Harris Clubhouse, a highly popular Club activity. Of them, former Secretary and Historian William Stark (President 1956-1957) wrote,

> Lively discussions in the little clubroom had been one of the chief attractions of the Club. When the new building was being planned, the possibility of providing for meetings small enough to permit general discussion was considered, but proposals to reduce the planned size of the auditorium or to divide it by a moveable partition received little support.

The Club, anticipating the need for more land at a future date, purchased two lots to the north of the property in February of 1951. These were lots #31 and #47 bounded by Park Avenue and Keyes Avenue. They were a section of the Morseland Gardens Subdivision and provided an additional eighty-six-foot-wide strip to the north of the original property. The purchase price was $5,000.

During the summer of 1955, air conditioning was added to the building. This was done at a cost of $10,000 (the money taken from reserves). It was thus possible to avoid special solicitation from the members.

The pattern that prevailed was to hold the general meetings and the larger interest group meetings in the Auditorium. A more informal give-and-take was usual among the smaller groups that met in the other rooms.

One room at the rear of the Auditorium was the small Library; the other was originally called the Card Room, and for many years there was not another designation. The various bridge groups met there for their games, though the room was also used for other scheduled group meetings: book reviews, philosophical discussions, and others. That room became the Gallery, and it is an important feature of the Clubhouse today. In 2010, the bridge players still met in that room at their scheduled times, surrounded by the art of the month.

With the acquisition of a large kitchen, the biweekly dinners became smoother in operation than had been the case when the food was served at one location, then members reassembled for the lecture at another. A caterer was employed, and group singing was engaged in while the tables were being cleared after dinner and before the lectures began. The recorded minutes indicate that these were convivial male affairs. The community singing, however, was eventually discontinued.

After the first twenty-five years, the building underwent a number of major changes, which included additions, renovations, and enhancements.

1970 — Remodeling

The House and Grounds Vice President's report at the Annual Meeting in March 1971 stated that "the first complete remodeling of the Club since our new Clubhouse was built" had taken place in the preceding months. Early in June of 1970, Billings McArthur (President 1966-1967) outlined to the Board the needs of the Club. Contracts were let in mid-July to renovate the air-conditioning system, paint the interior, install panic locks, and install new draperies and carpet. The total cost of those improvements amounted to somewhat less than the $14,000 authorized.

Space in the new building, however, was becoming a problem, and it was apparent that the Club would need to address that issue.

1971—Porch Enclosed

In early October of 1970, the Board approved the idea of an extension of the Library. Planners looked to the open porch on the north side of the building, outside the Card Room (now the Gallery) and the small Library (now the Reading Room). In February 1971, the renovation of that porch (which had been discussed at previous meetings) was authorized to proceed with an expenditure of up to $2,500, "such renovation to include a wooden floor on the porch." By March, the work on the porch was being completed, but the "complete remodeling" called for by the Committee report was not accomplished. The additional space provided a place for the Board and other committees to meet, but the improvements, while welcome, had done little to alleviate the need for enlarging the Library.

Funds had been set aside for an extension, and in July 1971 a Library Extension Committee was instructed to arrange with Architect J. Gamble Rogers to draw up plans and specifications. It was determined that the new stack space should be adjacent to the new Board and committee room space.

The original Library continued to grow, the interest groups proliferated, and the need for more space continued to be a problem. The popularity of the biweekly dinners often necessitated putting up tables in the Gallery and the small Library. Also, nine years after the first renovation, the interior of the building was again showing evidence of its hard use. Accordingly, an undertaking was launched that came to be known as Project Face Lift.

1979—Project Face Lift

A Steering Committee called an open meeting at the Club on March 21, 1979, to discuss the proposals for the Face Lift, which would include four projects:

- improvements to the auditorium involving replacement of the old acoustical ceiling and installation of new lighting and a new projection screen, new carpeting, and repainting the Auditorium;
- improving the office facilities;
- redecorating the ladies' room; and
- installing an underground irrigation system.

Monies would be raised by solicitation of members, and with the funds in hand, the changes began. By the summer of 1980, many of the proposed changes had been made and small items purchased or otherwise replaced.

1984 — Golden Flame

To prepare for the celebration of the Golden Anniversary of the Club in March of 1984, a 50th Anniversary Committee was formed in May of 1983. The Board minutes of September that year made the first mention of "Golden Flame for Club Improvement" and in October, a letter was sent to the membership soliciting funds for the Golden Flame. In that period, a bequest of $1,500 was received and the Golden Flame campaign eventually realized a total of $18,000. A substantial portion of that was spent on painting the interior and exterior of the building.

All the changes to the building were admired and enjoyed, but the persistent question of more space for the Library had not been addressed. At the May 6, 1985 meeting, the expansion of the Library was again proposed, with the suggestion that a small kitchen be included in the plans. No progress was made on either suggestion, however, until May of the following year, when the Board expressed its full agreement that the Building Committee should begin without delay to develop plans for a Library extension.

1986-87 — Library Addition

But it was more than a year later that the Building Committee was again directed to proceed at once with the business of getting plans for the long-discussed extension of the Library. Much consideration had been given to the possibility of also enlarging the Auditorium at the same time. This idea was discarded as being unfeasible and plans were submitted in the fall for a Library extension of fifty feet on the west side of the building, cutting two doors through the existing Library wall.

The Library Addition

In February 1987, the long-awaited Library addition was completed and ready for occupancy. The suggested other additions (enlarging the Auditorium, improving the kitchen, and adding another restroom) had not been achieved. The old small library became the Reading Room—a pleasant lounge with a table, several easy chairs, current periodicals— and some books. The addition, besides providing more room for the ever-growing collection of books, became a place for group meetings, committee sessions, and additional space for social groups, including rentals.

But other inadequacies of the Clubhouse became increasingly apparent. With the admission of women to membership in 1982, the small, inconvenient women's restroom had become a growing embarrassment. Much of the equipment in the kitchen was old and inefficient. The floor of the kitchen was showing evidence of trouble with the joists, presenting a safety hazard. More space was crucial to the operation of the office. The Boardroom was inadequate for the increasing business of the Club committees and the growing needs of the various interest groups. Storage space was inadequate. The men's restroom needed upgrading. It was obvious that the needed improvements could not be accomplished within the existing space of the Clubhouse.

1992—Boardroom Addition and Other Improvements

So in 1991, another building project was undertaken with the appointment of an *ad hoc* committee to study the needs, consult with an architect, develop plans, enlist the support of the membership, and obtain gifts and pledges. J. B. Lea (President 1991-1992) appointed Joe Terranova (President 1990-1991) as Chair of the committee, which included subcommittees composed of members who had special expertise in areas related to the responsibilities of each subcommittee. Club Member Donovan Allen was chosen as architect. Plans were drawn, submitted to the membership for approval, and ground was broken for the extensive project on May 26, 1992.

For this ground-breaking there was no super deluxe shovel borrowed from Rollins College, nor was there any long list of invited community dignitaries. No one waxed poetic. The President and some Past Presidents each took a turn at the shovel. The ground-breaking was especially significant to J. B. Lea, who had pushed so hard for the project, and for Joe Terranova, who had labored with the plans and with selling the project to the membership, later working long hours in a supervisory capacity while construction was in progress. The architect was present as well as the contractor, John Enslow. One of the City Commissioners, Rachel Murrah, was present. She had been extremely helpful in expediting some of the paper work with the city. And interested members and friends turned out to share the fun in the warm May sunshine.

The change was an addition to the north side of the building. The addition included arches to blend with the Gamble Rogers arches of the facade, a porch, and two entrance doors. The new space housed a large Board Room with an outside door to the new porch. The new women's and men's restrooms were well-equipped, tastefully décorated, and comfortably sized. The handicapped-access ramp on the west side of the building was replaced for better safety and convenience.

Boardroom Addition

The changes to the interior were dramatic, beginning just inside the Webster Avenue entrance. The antiquated ladies' room vanished and was relocated in the new addition beyond the Card Room/Gallery at the rear of the auditorium.

A small closet was built in part of the space inside the Webster Avenue entrance door. The Club office was enlarged by absorbing space that had been a cloak room. A door was cut through from the foyer to the kitchen, and a restroom for staff use was built in part of that space.

The kitchen was completely remodeled and upgraded with new equipment. The kitchen entry from the driveway was resurfaced and a convenience ramp was constructed for deliveries. After construction was well under way, the *Orlando Sentinel* reported in a story in the issue of June 11 that the University Club was "bringing the building into the '90s." The addition and renovations were completed in time for an Open House party in early November to celebrate the new look of the Clubhouse. The changes cost just over $235,000. No redecorating of the Auditorium and other existing rooms, however, was included.

Of considerable importance was the enlarging of the tool shed just west of the Clubhouse. The shed was too small to house all the equipment necessary for maintenance of the grounds, particularly the ride-on lawnmower. That machine had been inconveniently housed in the garage of Joe Terranova (President 1990-1991), a few houses away on Park Avenue, and had to be driven to and from the Clubhouse when the grass needed attention.

Of all the additions to the Clubhouse, this entire project was by far the most extensive — and expensive. Funds were raised by donations and pledges by the members, by a line of credit at the Barnett Bank, and by a grant from the Edyth Bush Charitable Foundation.

The changes to the Clubhouse had been accomplished without any interruption in the Club's programs. Rentals were not scheduled during that time but the activities groups met as scheduled, as did both the Friday afternoon general meetings and the Friday evening dinners. The Club staff and the contractors earned the gratitude of the entire membership for this feat.

2006-2008 — Audio-Visual

Under the leadership of Bob Reed (President 2007-2008) and House and Grounds Vice President Gordon Shepardson, several audio-visual enhancements were added to the Clubhouse starting in 2006. The whole building was rewired for sound and video amplification. More up-to-date wireless and wired microphones were purchased along with new speakers. Stage lighting was installed, with two spots and four flood lights mounted on the ceiling in front of the stage. A modern digital projector and a television camera were placed in the ceiling of the auditorium. A closed-circuit television (CCTV) system was acquired, capable of recording video programs and projecting TV pictures on the existing screen in the Auditorium and on new television monitors in the Gallery and the Library, with the potential of including a set in the Boardroom at a later date.

The audio-visual control room at the rear of the Auditorium, between the Gallery and the Reading Room, was filled to capacity, in order to accommodate the management of the equipment. These improvements served not only to augment presentations for Club activities, but also to enhance the rental potential.

In the years from 1934 to 2010, the University Club moved from a borrowed room at the Chamber of Commerce to the present commodious Clubhouse, with a stopover of a few years at the much-loved Little Harris Clubhouse. The founders would be pleased at the progress.

CHAPTER 5

The Clubhouse Grounds

Almost from the beginning, the grounds of the Clubhouse took on an entity of their own, apart from the building itself. The landscaping was — and still is — an ongoing project by the members.

The original plans for the utilization of the property, showing the location of sidewalks and driveway, were essentially as they are in 2010. The sidewalk, extending from the Park Avenue entrance (obviously intended by the architect to be the front door) bore no relation to the driveways.

Since there is no sidewalk on the west side of Park Avenue, the walk to the entrance connected at the corner with the sidewalk on the north side of Webster Street. The drive entered the property on the Webster (south) side, making the Webster side door the convenient entrance.

So the side door became the "front" door of the building and the planned front door became little used. The Park Avenue intended front door is used today as access to the flagpole for raising and lowering the flag, and to the new Gazebo. Some outdoor concerts and receptions are occasionally held on that lawn, but the Club has been an unfortunate victim of the weather, and many of the scheduled activities in recent years have been rained out.

Webster Avenue Entrance

The center of the parking lot was originally planned as an azalea garden, with cuttings to be taken from the plants and rooted for planting in other locations on the grounds. This plan withered away with time, and was replaced by two flowering trees, presented to the Club by Member Bill Williams, at that location behind the toolshed.

The original palm trees, which were the gift of Miss Genius when the clubhouse was built, long since lived out their life span and have disappeared.

The record suggests that in the beginning a few members took over the responsibility for maintaining and enhancing the grounds. However, because of the size of the property, professional lawn service became necessary. In 2010, nearly all the yard work is handled by a lawn service under the direction of the House and Grounds Vice President and the Facilities Manager. Many members, however, have taken a great interest in the landscaping of the property over the years and have contributed time and money to that cause.

In 1971 the Club was blessed when a professional landscape architect retired to Winter Park and soon became a member — Frederick W. Short. He gave an account of the years following 1971.

> At the University Club we pride ourselves on being a do-it-yourself organization. It was this feature that first attracted me to the group when I was approached by Vic Gardner (President 1962-1963) to become a member of his Landscaping Committee to help keep the grounds neat and presentable and worthy of the great occasions that constantly transpire therein.
>
> The grounds were graced by many citrus trees, one huge oak, and four towering but weak-wooded silk oaks, which soon became a nuisance. One by one these were removed.
>
> It was evident that a comprehensive general plan and a sprinkler system were needed so Member Arthur Ullman, a Harvard graduate landscape architect, and I drew up a general plan.
>
> Soon things began to happen. Overgrown shrubbery and hedges were removed or replaced according to the approved plan. William Mackinnon, Frank Linn (President 1974-1975), Edward Andrews, and others each added their expertise, while Billings McArthur (President 1966-1967), with his hobby of collecting and propagating all kinds of exotic trees and shrubs collected while traveling abroad, added to our enthusiasm.
>
> It was usual during the winter months to see a large basket of grapefruit or oranges by the front porch for members to help themselves as they left the meetings.
>
> The common bond was a yen to plant, cultivate, pull weeds, and see the grounds and the Clubhouse evolve in pace with the stimulating programs we have become accustomed to enjoying. We believed there was nothing degrading about blue jeans, work gloves, and the use of the good supply of garden tools from the toolshed.

In fact, the scanty funds and the all-male membership were all the incentive needed.

Over the years, changes were inevitable, but the golden *tabebuia unbellata* propagated from seed gathered in the Orient and planted in McArthur's memory some time after his death serves as one of the many reminders surrounding our beautiful clubhouse.

The high cost of irrigating the extensive grounds had, over the years, escalated to a point of being of considerable concern to the Board. Accordingly, in conjunction with the remodeling and expansion of the Clubhouse undertaken in 1992, a well was drilled to a depth of 255 feet on Club property and a five-horsepower submersible pump was installed. As Member G. Elliott Smith wrote,

> The entire system has been amortized in slightly less than two years and henceforth will provide an annual saving of over $2,500 as compared to the current cost of an equivalent quantity of water from the City of Winter Park. This advantage is certain to widen as the cost of government services continues to escalate.

Eighteen years later, the well continued to provide water for the irrigation system, saving the Club tens of thousands of dollars over the years, with the prospect of even more in the future.

Following the building expansion of 1992, the House and Grounds Committee oversaw the planting of many attractive annuals, especially near the Webster Street entrance. In 1994 the grounds were further beautified by the addition of nineteen pine trees near the north boundary of the property, the gift of John Newell, then-Chair of the Committee.

One feature of the grounds is the sign by the driveway into the property from the Webster Street entrance. This handsome sign identifies the property. It is also an illustration of the early hands-on work of Club members.

Virgil Hartsock (President 1981-1982) was deeply involved in this project, and his account of the design and construction of the sign is a saga in Club history:

> It was during the summer of 1975 when Frank Linn, President, asked me to replace the wooden No Parking sign at the Webster Street entrance. That sign was weather-beaten and askew because of loss of footing. I explained that I had done some woodworking but had no experience in making a sign suitable for the Club. And as we talked, the project grew from a No Parking sign to a permanent University Club sign.
>
> I contacted my friend, member, and noted artist Charles Turzak, explaining the project to him. He was pleased to make conception drawings of various ideas for signs. He drew proposals to be made of brick and concrete. The Executive Board selected the drawing using concrete and decorative concrete blocks. ...
>
> I then began to design in detail the many charts and diagrams for the construction of the sign. My wife, Mary, made templates of hard cardboard for the letters. After the detailed designs were made I began the woodwork. With the templates, I cut the letters from one-half-inch plywood with an angled edge cut. The letters were fine-sanded and the mold form was built.

Approval for the sign construction was given by the City of Winter Park early in February 1976, ground was broken, and the footer was poured. Reinforcement rods were installed to ensure that the sign could not be pushed over.

Later, during the widening of Webster Avenue, the City moved the sign to the Park Avenue side of the Clubhouse; it was then replaced on its original site after the road work was completed. Thanks to the sound construction and care used by the City, the sign never showed that it had been temporarily uprooted.

First Sign

Second Sign

The original sign itself consisted of a concrete slab resting on a base of decorative blocks with "University Club" lettering. However, after nearly thirty-five years of exposure to the Florida sun and rain, it showed signs of wear and needed to be replaced. In 2007 three generous donors contributed $1500 toward the purchase of a handsome Brazilian granite slab with prominent words:

UNIVERSITY CLUB of Winter Park

The white decorative blocks from the original sign were retained and only the top portion was replaced with the granite slab. Later, the blocks were stained to match the granite. Installed in 2008, the sign is an attractive addition to the Clubhouse grounds.

While the Clubhouse grounds had been well kept, the years had taken their toll. In his remarks upon being elected President of the Club in 2008, Frank Paul Barber proposed a complete renovation of the landscaping of the Club, including the sprinkler system. The project would be financed by donations from members and the campaign generated more than $45,000 over two years. Once donations began, a committee was formed, a landscape architect was hired, and ground was broken.

The plan called for a phased project to take advantage of the funds as they were donated. Five phases were planned, with new plants and trees and some special features.

Phase #1 The south exposure (Webster Avenue).

Phase #2 The east exposure (Park Avenue). A Veterans Memorial surrounding the flag pole was planned with engravable pavers installed to honor Club members who served in the military. They could be purchased for $100.

Landscaping Groundbreaking 2009

Phase #3   The north exposure (adjoining private home). Includes a Gazebo, dedicated to Murrell Copeland, the wife of Club Member Bob Copeland, donated in her honor. The Gazebo is intended for rentals — weddings and other events. This area may also contain engravable pavers that can be used to mark the occasion of its use.

Phase #4   The west exposure (facing the parking area). Contains a decorative fountain, dedicated to a major donor. Surrounding it are three benches dedicated to donors with engravable pavers.

Phase #5   The parking area. Contains fifteen live Oak trees that can be purchased for $2,000 to honor someone chosen by the donor. Surrounding the perimeter will be a bush line to delineate the property line.

The purchase of the trees and pavers are planned to provide an income stream to fund the upkeep of the landscaping and other landscaping enhancements.

By 2010 the first four phases were completed and the work continued. The Clubhouse now enjoys a beautiful renewed setting.

The Fountain

The Gazebo

PART II

CHAPTER 6

Governance and Leadership

As mentioned earlier, the founders of the Club thought that the group could function informally without much organizational structure, but the need for officers and bylaws quickly arose. After having had just one presiding officer and only three meetings over a period of nine months in 1934, a President and a Secretary-Treasurer were elected and a constitution was proposed and adopted a short time later. By the spring of 1935 a formal organization was emerging.

An application for a charter was granted by the Circuit Court, only to have a lawyer-member point out that legally the Club did not exist, because there were no bylaws to list the provisions for election of officers. The deficiency was rectified and the legal existence and entity of the University Club of Winter Park was established in 1941.

The first Charter and Bylaws are in Appendix A. But the basic governance of the organization took shape and prevailed for many years. It consisted of a President, First Vice President for Programs, Second Vice President for House and Grounds, Third Vice President for Finance, Fourth Vice President for Membership, a Secretary, and a Treasurer. It became traditional for the First Vice President to succeed the President—although this did not always happen. The composition of the Board was determined by the Bylaws. The new Bylaws that were approved in 1977 contained many standing rules.

Following the threat of the withdrawal of the tax exemption in 1980, the Charter was revised in 1982 to more clearly state the objectives of the Club and bring them into line with the requirements of Chapter 501(c)(3) of the Tax Code and current corporate practice. The composition of the Board became determined by the Charter.

The Club, though, is governed by the membership through its elected officers. The members have the final determination on any matter, which is expressed by their votes at the Annual Meeting. Over the years, there have been at least three gatherings that have elicited strong feelings and discussion by the members. Most were involved with the criteria for membership in the Club.

(1) In 1947, the members engaged in vigorous debate over the site for the Clubhouse; the votes were close. And later there were proposed Bylaw changes to (2) admit women members (1981), and (3) admit corporate members (2007). The first two were approved after spirited debate but the third was tabled in similar circumstances.

The Charter and Bylaws were also amended in 1993 to eliminate the titles of the vice presidents and to add the positions of Assistant Treasurer and three Directors-at-Large. Bylaw amendments were again made in 1994 to create initiation fees and spouse memberships. In 1998 the Charter was again amended to eliminate the designated Vice-President positions and replace them with the phrase "four or more vice presidents." The same four designated positions were created in the Bylaws.

The position Vice President of Development was created in 2003 in the Bylaws, and in 2006 the position of Vice President of Intellectual Activities was added. The Bylaws were again extensively revised in 2008 and the position of Executive Vice President added.

Bob Wilkinson (President 1980-1981) and Virgil Hartsock (President 1981-1982) inherited the IRS problem in 1980 and shepherded the successful transition of the Club to conform to government tax rules and regulations, with changes in the Charter and Bylaws (see Chapter 7). And for more than twenty-four years, Wilkinson has served the Board as Parliamentarian. In that role, he has given wise advice and council to that body at their meetings and authored the many other Charter and Bylaw changes for consideration by the members at the annual membership meetings. In addition, his institutional memory has provided the Board with accurate information and the perspective for them to make sound and reasoned decisions.

In 2007, Wilkinson undertook the task of examining all the Bylaws, making proposed changes to eliminate outdated ones and many that were contradictory or duplicates. The many changes were approved by the members at the Annual Meeting in 2008. Some of the older members quipped that "while we're at it, we should consider making some changes to the Bill of Rights."

Wilkinson was honored by the Board at his retirement from that body in 2010 by the presentation of a Plaque of Recognition, noting his long and loyal service to the Club. He continues to serve as Parliamentarian in 2010.

The Club has been well served in its governance by its leaders. In its 75-year history, seventy-one Presidents have led the Club.

While there have been a few contentious annual membership and Board meetings over the years, the Club, as Don Meckstroth (President 1995-1996) has always maintained, is a "culture of civility" in Club matters. This has been responsible for progressive leadership and accomplishments by the Presidents during their tenures. Some of these are discussed here.

J. B. Lea served as President in 1991-1992. He was successful in obtaining a $45,000 matching grant from the Edyth Bush Charitable Foundation to be used for the 1992-1994 renovation and addition to the Club. A survey of new members who had resigned from the Club about this time revealed that they left because they found the Club unfriendly. In an effort to change this perception, he made several changes:

- He replaced the long rectangular tables with round ones, which improved conversation and sociability during luncheons and dinners.
- He introduced the social hour for wine and fellowship before each dinner.
- He hired Leona Paul and her son, George, of Classic Creations to cater the dinners.

Round Tables

For many years, in honor of the holiday season, the Club's Auditorium and Christmas tree were beautifully decorated by J. B., assisted by his wife, Barbara, much to the enjoyment of Club members and guests.

During the Don Meckstroth presidenial term (1995-1996), the Club established a General Endowment Fund when former Member H. Gerald Smith bequeathed a large sum for this purpose. This has helped keep dues increases relatively modest. A "quiet" membership campaign was successful in keeping the membership stable, and the profile of the desired members in those years was "a retired or near-term executive, manager, or professional."

While the additions to the Clubhouse were accomplished in 1994, no renovation of the auditorium was included. Richard Sewell (President 1996-1998), however, presided over the redecorating of the auditorium, drawing on donations from the membership. Member Elizabeth Von Rieben, a professional interior decorator, led that committee, and a new Masland carpet was installed in July 1997—lasting until replacement became necessary in 2010.

Dick Artz (President 1998-1999) recruited and managed the new staff during this period and established new rental procedures and initiatives, which resulted in the doubling of income from that source, and the first Operating Procedures Manual was written. This document describes the purpose of the many committees and other duties and responsibilities of Club leadership. It was written by the members in charge of those duties at that time. He encouraged spouses to become full members. University Club license plates were acquired during his tenure, and more University

Club blazer patches were obtained. Both were offered for sale at a modest price, and helped promote the Club. His green-and-white magnetic name badges had been acquired earlier.

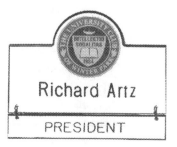

Richard Artz

PRESIDENT

Elizabeth Brothers was eminently qualified to be the first woman admitted to membership in 1981, and even more so when, eighteen years later, she was selected to be the first woman to preside over the Club (1999-2000). She had been recruited as Development Director at Rollins College by Club Member and Rollins President Thaddeus Seymour. And she had also put her outreach and fund-raising experience to good use as Vice President Development. She served the Club well, and her mantra was, "No contribution is too large." When asked about her term of office, she remarked, "There are two valuable benefits [*to the presidency*]: a reserved parking place and a guaranteed reservation for all dinner meetings!"

Bill Munsie (President 2000-2001) arranged for the recovery of the "New York Bay" wood block mural (described in Chapter 14), which had been stored in a member's house, and had it installed in the auditorium. Also, during his tenure, the Board established a retirement program for the staff.

Further progress was made during the administration of the second woman to head the organization, Diane Sandquist (President 2001-2002). Under her leadership, the Club "sailed along," and applied for and received the state sales tax exemption.

President George Wannall (2002-2003) created fiscal policies that resulted in a small budget surplus at the end of that fiscal year. But the number of new members was becoming insufficient to replace those who resigned, moved away, or died.

The Board and Club members were apprised of the problem of declining membership and income by Fred Rosenthal (President 2003-2004), who developed a profile of the Club for discussion at an all-day seminar for the Board. Some long-range planning was developed during his tenure. In cooperation with Rollins College, he also created the Preceptor Program in which Club members provide their expertise in specific subjects to classes at the college. This was expanded in 2009 by adding a Club Speakers Service.

Dan Schulz (President 2004-2006) served two one-year terms. During that period, the concern for new members continued. An additional problem was a downturn in the stock market in the previous three years, resulting in reduced income from that source.

Although facing a budget deficit, the Board chose not to raise dues. Instead, they increased the price of lunches and dinners, sufficient to balance the budget. But the Club experienced roof and tree damage in three hurricanes that occurred in a four-week period. The Club was forced to close for two weeks and the Board had to dig into its reserves to accommodate the budget. During the second Schulz term, the Club established the Amigo program to welcome, monitor, and nurture new members. But in spite of cost-cutting that included the elimination of a House and Grounds position, deficits continued to climb, and the dues had to be increased by $75 (to $275) for regular members.

In an effort to increase the membership by making the Club more open in the nighttime hours to prospective members, Joe Rizzo (President 2006-2007) established two evening Intellectual Activities—a second Current Events group and a Writers Group in association with the Florida Writers Association. He also set the stage for a later, very successful, Classical Music day program. During his watch, a proposal to admit corporations as members was approved by the Board, but a subsequent Bylaw change to do so was tabled at the annual membership meeting.

There was no increase in member dues during the next administration of Bob Reed (President 2007-2008). Under the leadership of Frank Paul Barber, Vice President of Development that year, there was a greater increase in individual donations than at any time in the previous thirteen years. A successful 90-Day Campaign brought in ninety-eight new members, the most in recent memory. The Club's interior and exterior were painted, the parking lot was paved, high-top tables were purchased, and the closed circuit television system was completed. An extensive rewriting of the Operations Manual coordinated by Member Joe Smith was accomplished that year, as well as a revision of many of the Bylaws by Parliamentarian Bob Wilkinson (President 1980-1981), as noted earlier. A Rental Policies *ad hoc* Committee was created and the Human Resources Committee rewrote staff job descriptions.

Frank Paul Barber served as President in 2008-2009. During his tenure, extensive plans were developed for the improvement of the landscaping of the Club and a very successful campaign to create funds to achieve this undertaking brought in $45,000 (see Chapter 5). Barber also created three new Intellectual Activities: Health and Wellness, Legacy Writing, and Loss Support.

During Barber's tenure, the Club began the celebration of its 75 Years with special events that included an ArtFest, a MusicFest, a WineFest, and an Open House. The Men's Chorus created an anniversary concert consisting of "75 Songs for 75 Years in 75 Minutes," and the Mayor of Winter Park designated April 4, 2009 as "The University Club of Winter Park Day." Continued membership losses, however, required the Board to raise the dues by $25 (to $300) for regular members and to $150 for Spouse Members. The membership also approved the creation of the position of Executive Vice President, which was filled by Max Reed.

She became the third woman president in 2009-2010, and continued the celebrations of the 75th Anniversary by appointing an *ad hoc* 75th Anniversary Committee with Diane Sandquist (President 2001-2002) as Coordinator. As the year proceeded, a banner weekend in cooperation with Rollins College (celebrating its 150th anniversary) was undertaken. Featuring faculty and music staff from Rollins, a special luncheon was held honoring the Bach Festival and the Rollins faculty. Leaders of the long-running Financial Lunches and the Presidents Emeriti were also honored. And in a cooperative venture with the British-American Chamber of Commerce and the Central Florida Branch of the English-Speaking Union, a garden party was held on a sunny October afternoon on the lawns of the Club.

It became an unwritten tradition that the President of the Club would serve for only one year. It is uncertain where this concept arose, although it was indirectly suggested by Dr. Whicher, the first Chairman, during the first year when there were few meetings. (It was noted earlier that he strenuously vetoed the suggestion that the presiding officer be named The Factotum.) He served as Chairman for a few meetings, then was elected President (1935-1936) for the succeeding full year. Since then, the one-year tradition has held, with a few notable exceptions.

William Trufant Foster (1950) unfortunately died in office; Clarence M. Day filled out the unexpired term and was elected President in 1951, serving until 1952. Three other men served two consecutive years. Lester Schriver 1970-1972), J. Richard Sewell (1996-1998) and Dan Schulz (2004-2006). Two Presidents served two nonconsecutive terms, John Milton Moore (1938-1939 and 1942-1943) and David Stonecliff (1988-1989 and 1994-1995).

There have been three women Presidents (M. Elizabeth Brothers (1999-2000), Diane Sandquist (2001-2002), and Max Reed (2009-2010). One couple has served as President at two different times: Bob Reed (2007-2008) and Max Reed (2009-2010). Most of the recent Presidents are still active members of the Club. (See Appendix D.)

During the 75 years of the Club, a close bond developed among the Presidents Emeriti. Quipping that their leadership resulted in the receipt of the "top dollar" for their services, they began the tradition of the annual Spring Past Presidents' Lunches in the 1970s. Hosted by the current President, the luncheon introduces the incoming President to the group and is followed by reminiscences, tall tales, and harmonious camaraderie. The Council of Presidents Emeriti continues to meet and give advice to the current President and the Executive Board, as needed.

Some of the other officers and committee chairs have had longer tenures and have contributed to the Club's ongoing progress. The continuity of Club governance is a tribute to its loyal members.

The Committees—standing, special, and *ad hoc*—are the heart of the organization. Because the University Club is an organization of volunteers with only a small full-time paid staff, much of the work is done by the members who offer a multitude of talented expertise. Ken Murrah (a member since 1963) has provided *pro bono* legal council and sound advice to the leadership on many matters. Another outstanding example is the dedicated volunteer work of Member Pat Curenton who, from the late 1990s has contributed many hours of time assisting the office staff, as well as heading the Craft Group, the Amigos, and the After Hours Committee. For several years, she sat on the Board as the Assistant Treasurer, and she has served on the Program Committee. But her most important contribution may be as the leader of the Seating Committee at lunches and dinner, for without her, no one would know where to sit!

The progression from a single committee for programs after the first year in 1934 to the present forty-two committees and thirty plus intellectual activity groups is astonishing. (See Appendix C.)

CHAPTER 7

Tax-Exempt Status

A complication of the Club's organization has been the oc-casionally recurring question of tax-exempt status with both the local and Federal governments.

From the beginning, the members viewed their Club as a charitable and educational organization. William Stark (President 1956-1957) wrote of this in *The First Twenty-Five Years*.

> The term "university club" tends to give a false im-pression of the nature of our association. Some persons hearing the term may picture an exclusive social club. It required time and effort to correct the misunder-standing.

When application was made to the IRS for exemption from income tax on receipts from dues, it was first denied on the grounds that this was a social club. But a request for reconsid-eration, supported by copies of the Charter and Bylaws and a complete set of Club programs, was successful in obtaining (in November 1944) a classification as an educational organi-zation and exempt from Federal income tax.

When the present Clubhouse was erected in 1948 the tax problem arose again, this time with the City of Winter Park. More than a year of anxiety and effort passed before the City Commission ruled on April 19, 1949 that exemption from taxes be granted as long as the Club continued to maintain its program of literary, educational, and charitable purposes.

Without these tax exemptions it would have been impossible for the Club to hold to its policy of keeping the dues low. Recognizing that the exemptions were granted because of the nature of the purposes and programs, the officers of the Club did not encourage the introduction of activities of a purely social or recreational nature. Then a devastating complication arose in the form of letters received in 1979 from a member.

A fine account of the contretemps was prepared by Virgil L. Hartsock (President 1981-1982) and the following résumé of the events is his, edited to comply with existing documents.

1979-1983 Tax Exempt Status

1. On March 28, 1979, Mr. Winthrop A. Wilson, a member of the University Club of Winter Park tried to cause the Executive Committee of the University Club of Winter Park to defer a proposed expenditure of $35,000 until after a review of the Club's tax-exemption status. Mr. Wilson was concerned that the Club had become a "private social club." He believed that the Club was not organized and operated exclusively for educational and charitable purposes.

2. During April 1979 five letters were received from Mr. Wilson on the subject of tax exemption. Mr. Gil Buhrmann (President 1978-1979) responded to Mr. Wilson that a complete review would be made regarding his concern by Mr. John F. Varian, Attorney at Law.

3. On June 13, 1979 Mr. Wilson wrote letters to Mr. Roy Parrish, Director, Ad Valorem Tax Division, Florida Department of Revenue and Mr. Charles DeWitt, District Director of Internal Revenue. Mr. Wilson stated that the University Club of Winter Park does not qualify as a 501(c)(3) Tax Exempt educational and charitable organization. It was his contention that the Club be reclassified as a Social Organization.

4. On June 15, 1979 Mr. Varian responded to the Club (Mr. Gil Buhrmann, President; Mr. Weldon B. Manwaring, Club Auditor; and Mr. Clyde Bloxsom, Treasurer.)

5. *During June through August much correspondence flowed and discussions were held regarding Mr. Wilson's attempts to alter the Club's tax-exempt status. Mr. William B. Edmands (President 1979-1980) presented the problem to Mr. William A. Walker II, Attorney with Winderweedle, Haines, Ward and Woodman, P.A. Mr. Walker replied that we should do nothing until we hear from the IRS.*

6. *On January 27, 1980 the University Club received a formal letter from the IRS dated January 25, 1980 proposing the withdrawal of the Club's 501(c)(3) tax exempt status. The letter was signed by Sherry W. Hallihan, E. O. Specialist of the IRS, Jacksonville Florida District. The letter generalized the findings stated by Ms. Hallihan on January 22, 1980 at a meeting at the University Club with Mr. Weldon B. Manwaring. Ms. Hallihan had previously examined the activities of the Club and the records for the year ending April 30, 1978. She stated that the Club's donations were much too small for a 501(c)(3) tax-exempt status and barely enough to qualify for a 501(c)(4) status. The Club has accumulated sizeable funds for no specific purpose. The Club did not open its doors to the public. The University Club is a closed "men only" organization not operating for charitable and educational purposes under 501(c)(3) rules. The Club permits special privileges to certain members, such as some pay full dues while others pay reduced dues or no dues, yet enjoy the same Club benefits.*

501(c)(4) Tax Exempt Status: Members have received certain privileges such as public (dinners), but no members may be privileged as to others (low dues or no dues). Pow Wows, bridge, camera, etc. must be open to an actively solicited public. Gifts from members and others must be clearly segregated and accounted for in order to be deducted by donors. Club donations must be sizeable, at present deemed very small.

501(c)(7) Tax Exempt Status - Basically a social Club could escape taxation on certain gifts by setting up a private foundation to house this income taxable at two percent. Unrelated income over a certain percentage of gross from other operations would be taxed at corporate rates. This would apparently also mean giving all our present funds to a foundation.

Taxable profit and loss would be computed as for a corporation, and would be taxed in a like manner. IRS would have no say as to how the Club invested its funds, spent income there from, or barred participation of the public. Since the Club's profits are small, it would be easy to legally not generate any taxable income. Gifts by donors not deductible by the donor.

7. Mr. William B. Edmands (President 1979-1980) established the Club Legal Advisory Committee composed of Mr. Edmands, Mr. William Walker II, Mr. David R. Roberts, Mr. Clifford Lee, Mr. John Varian, and Mr. Ralph McDermid. The Legal Advisory Committee agreed to consider and make known to the membership the following:

a.   Statements by Club to members regarding deductibility of current contributions.

b.   Treatment of current contributions to the Club.

c. Position taken by IRS Agent Hallihan.

d.   Technical strengths and weaknesses in the IRS position.

e.   Short-term response to IRS

f.   Long-term recommendations to the Club membership.

8. After much study and research a meeting in October 1980 was held with Mr. William Walker, Mr. Bill Edmands (Immediate Past President), and the current President, Mr. Bob Wilkinson (1980-1981) to review the present status of the Club's position and possible effects of changes. The results of this meeting were presented to the Executive Board of The University Club, which resists changes to the 501(c)(3) tax exempt status. On December 12, 1980 the Executive Board agreed to initiate new programs oriented toward public participation

9. Mr. Bob Wilkinson (President 1980-1981) initiated new programs oriented to public participation in December 1980. Work was started to review and revise where necessary the Club Bylaws, Charter, and Articles of Reincorporation. This action was to update our documentation and to include some additions to emphasize the nature of our Community oriented activity. Mr. Wilkinson requested Mr. Walkers' assistance in these matters.

10. *February 24, 1981 the revised University Club Charter was sent to IRS agent Hallihan.*

11. *At the regular Annual Meeting on March 6, 1981, President Bob Wilkinson presented to the membership the changes believed necessary by the Legal Advisory Committee, discussed and received a majority vote from the Past Presidents Council, and approved by the Executive Board. These proposed changes included:*

    a. Update the Club Charter and Bylaws
    b. Increase the "Open Door" policy to make the Club more available
    c. Permit women who meet established requirements to join the Club
    d. Discontinue the practice of permitting certain members who had limited income to continue enjoying full membership participation, even though a portion of the members dues were paid by another member.

12. *On October 23, 1981 Ms. M. Elizabeth Brothers was voted into full membership as the first woman to join The University Club.*

13. *It was becoming increasingly difficult for The University Club to operate under the cloud of the IRS Tax Exempt problem. Virgil Hartsock (President 1981-1982) presented to the Executive Board the efforts made by the Club to satisfy the major problems stated by the IRS and said that time was passing without resolution. The Executive Board agreed that the problem had been with us too long and efforts should be made to resolve the matter. On October 27, 1981 a letter was sent to Mr. William Walker II, Club Attorney, giving the conclusions of the Executive Board and requesting a meeting between Ms. Sherry W. Hallihan, her supervisor, and Mr. William A. Walker to reach an agreement on the Tax Exempt problem. It was further requested that Mr. Walker while establishing the meeting, determine the back-up information believed necessary to satisfy the request for continued 501(c)(3) tax exempt status by The University Club.*

14. *On December 16, 1981 Mr. Hartsock (President 1981-1982), forwarded to Mr. Walker, Club Attorney, a complete analysis and*

comments on the IRS Report of Examination for Club activities for the year ending April 30, 1978. Also included were copies of past Club Time (the Club's newsletter) that included our scheduled activities to prove the fact that in the main, the Club's activities were educational, cultural, and literary. It also identified those activities that included other-than-members' participation. A number of newspaper clippings were included to show the Club activities that included other-than-members' participation and to show the Club activities where the public were invited to participate. A listing of Club rentals was furnished to identify the use of the Club by other Civic or Educational organizations (at cost only) and other community organizations or people. This information was compiled by Mr. Everett Hales (President 1982-1983) and Mr. Virgil Hartsock (President 1981-1982) through research of all old Club records and joint analysis. This letter and the enclosures were designed for the use of Mr. Walker in his meeting with the IRS as requested in the October 27, 1981 letter.

15. On February 8, 1983 The University Club of Winter Park received official notice that our 501(c)(3) tax exempt status was confirmed by Mr. Philip D. Myers, Jr., Appeals Officer, IRS Regional Commissioner, Atlanta, Georgia. Much gratitude and appreciation were given to the Club's Presidents, Mr. William Edmands, Mr. Bob Wilkinson, Mr. Virgil Hartsock and Mr. Everett Hales, their Executive Boards; the Legal Advisory Committee (especially Mr. William Walker, II, Club Attorney), and Mr. David Roberts for their efforts in bringing this case to a successful conclusion.

Mr. Walker, a member of the Club, provided his services over this prolonged period on a *pro bono* basis. His help was invaluable.

While the worrisome matters of Federal tax exemption were occurring, much soul searching was going on among the officers and the members. Perhaps the scope of the Club had been less broad than the members had believed. Perhaps the outreach to the community had been too limited. Perhaps, indeed, the Club had become more elitist and sexist. Perhaps the Club had from the beginning been elitist. Many interested members participated in the discussion and sought ways to remove any question from the Club's tax-free status, for without it the Club could not afford to exist.

President Virgil Hartsock, a civic leader who served on the Winter Park Centennial Celebration Committee and worked with the Rollins College Centennial Committee, also wrote the following.

> This was an excellent time to invite the general public to The University Club. Pictures of Past Presidents of Rollins College decorated the walls of The University Club as a part of the Winter Park Centennial. Other items the City Commission believed should be on display were placed on view at the Club. Hartsock requested that The University Club be made a part of the scheduled tours during the week of the Centennial Celebration. Members of the Club were hosts to the tours and discussed the displayed items and explained Club activities and toured all Club rooms.

New approaches were undertaken. At a meeting between Virgil Hartsock and Member Dave Roberts, it was suggested that the Winter Park Financial Luncheon Group be moved from its present meeting place (Harrigan's Restaurant) to the University Club as a new special interest group. After much discussion, the University Club Executive Board approved the acceptance of the Financial Luncheon Group, sponsored by the Edyth Bush Charitable Foundation, the Charles Hosmer Morse Foundation, Rollins College, the Winter Park Library, and the Club. Much later, this group of sponsors was joined by the Chamber of Commerce

This action doubled the size of the previous Financial Luncheon Group attendance, opened the doors of the Club to the public, and gave the Club an excellent opportunity for new members. All Intellectual Activity groups were encouraged to invite the public to their meetings. Announcements of the meetings of the Activities were given to local newspapers for publication as well as to local radio and television civic news announcements.

The changes made to the Charter and Bylaws brought changes to Club activities. The major change was the admission of women to membership and the active recruitment of African-Americans. The Clubhouse was made available to other nonprofit organizations on either a *pro bono* or a cost-of-use basis.

Club meetings, both general and those of the interest groups, were opened to the public, except for the biweekly dinners and the bridge groups, which remained members-and-guests-only activities. Cooperation by the Club with other nonprofit organizations devoted to promoting community concerns was increased.

The changes were not without problems, including downright resentment among a vocal few of the members. The decades since those events of the early 1980s, however, have brought added scope and richness to the programs and purposes of the Club.

With the termination of the Powwows in the eighties, much greater emphasis was placed on the expansion of the Activity groups and a new position of Vice President Intellectual Activities was created in 2004. There are now more than thirty of these groups covering a wide range of intellectual activities at which the public is welcome. Some are small but others draw a large number of participants.

The weekly Current Events group regularly draws a large audience — often as many as sixty. Recently Classical Music, a series of evening debates, and an Opera series have also had good attendance, both from members and the public. Others, including the Book Review and the Philosophical Discussion groups have been in existence since the early days of the Club.

Members of the Club continue to occasionally discuss and debate its purpose and emphasis in the new century. But the members in 2010 still embrace the concept of an educational-nonprofit entity that is dedicated to the Club motto *Intellectio Sodalitas* (Fellowship in Knowledge and Understanding.)

The Club is not a social organization or one that promotes business interchange and "networking." Nor is it a social gathering of like-minded individuals.

It is, rather, an institution dedicated to the advancement of knowledge as a lifelong pursuit, through the interchange of thoughts and ideas. It continues to adhere to the objectives of its founders of 75 years ago.

CHAPTER 8

Bequests, Gifts, and Investments

At the time of the founding of the Club in 1934, there was little need for money. The meeting-room was provided by the Chamber of Commerce, which also paid for postage and stationery. The largest expense during the first year or two was for mailing, because nearly all the members had permanent residences elsewhere.

Annual dues were set at one dollar, but were very soon raised to two dollars. Out of the money collected, a token sum was paid to the Chamber of Commerce in recognition of its support. It was the stated intention of the founders to keep the dues low so as not to prevent men of modest means from participating in the Club.

With the rapid growth of membership in the early years, new meeting space had become a necessity. As previously noted the Little Harris Clubhouse addition to the Country Club was built and paid for by a member as a surprise for the members when they returned in the fall of 1937.

The decision to build a new Clubhouse after World War II required much more money. And once again the members responded to the need; donations and pledges of $60,000 were soon received. A loan of $20,000 was obtained but this was quickly paid off as pledges came in. With the opening of the new building in 1948, costs increased considerably with the need for additional staff and maintenance of the building.

The 1992-1994 major renovation of the Club included the much-improved rest rooms and kitchen as well as the addition of a Boardroom. This ambitious major project was aided by a generous $45,000 matching grant from the Edyth Bush Charitable Foundation and a bequest of $60,000 from the estate of Club member Robert Highleyman. The balance of the needed funds was again provided by a bank loan and generous donations from members.

The Club has also been the beneficiary of substantial bequests from the estates of other deceased members. These have ranged from modest amounts to the Drey bequest exceeding one million dollars.

Bequests

In 1994 a bequest of $60,000 was received from the estate of H. Gerald Smith, a retired Foreign Service officer. (Smith had presented many programs at the Club about his experiences and travels.) Don Meckstroth (President 1995-1996) suggested that it be used to create a General Endowment fund, the earnings from which would be used to support Club operations. This was approved by the Board. Over the years the fund has grown to about $150,000 as unrestricted donations and bequests have been added to it.

Jessie Drey

In 1995 a remarkable bequest of more than one million dollars was received from the estate of Jessie and Eugene Drey. Jessie was born in London in 1904 of Scottish parents and was trained as a nurse. In 1935 she married an American stockbroker from St. Louis and they settled in Jersey in the Channel Islands. With the start of World War II in 1939, they moved to the United States. They returned to Jersey after the war but found their home in ruins so, once again, they moved back to the United States. When her husband retired in 1950 they settled in Winter Park but he died a few years later.

Mrs. Drey became very active in several of the local charitable organizations—soon after women were admitted to the Club, she became a member. On her death, the substantial estate was divided among the several organizations in which she had been so interested. The bequest to the Club created the Eugene and Jessie Drey Endowment, with the earnings contributing to Club operating costs and keeping dues increases to a minimum. Mrs. Drey was honored by the Board in 2008 with the naming of the Library "The Drey Library." Without income from the two funds—the General Endowment and the Drey Endowment—dues by 2010 would have been some sixty percent higher.

From the early days, two other funds have existed to support the mission of the Club, in accordance with the Charter. These are the Education Assistance fund dedicated to supporting students at institutions of higher learning and the Community Assistance fund to provide income to support deserving nonprofit organizations in Winter Park and the surrounding area.

A bequest of $10,000 from the estate of Walter Zimmerman was divided between the two funds. He was for many years the editor of *Club Time*. These funds have been built up over the years with contributions from members and bequests. Grants are made each year, with earnings from the funds supplemented by donations from members.

A bequest of $40,000 was received from the estate of John and Margaret Bennette to provide grants for students at Rollins College, the University of Central Florida, and Valencia Community College.

Other funds have been created through bequests to support the maintenance and improvement of the building and landscaping. A bequest of $100,000 was received from the estate of Elizabeth Edmands, the wife of William Edmands (President 1979-1980), to be used for improvement of the building and grounds.

Another bequest of $25,000 was received from the estate of Zena Brereton, a very active Club member, also for building and grounds.

Other significant bequests have been received from the estates of Charles and Faith Duffy ($35,000), Lorene Banta ($10,000), Germaine Haserot ($25,000), Dorothy and George Lee ($10,000), and Raymond Baker and Carolyn Shinkle ($15,000). All of these bequests contained no restrictions on their use.

Gifts

Almost from the beginning, there has been a compassionate concern for those who might find the dues a barrier to membership. Accordingly it had long been the practice for some members to anonymously pay part or all of the dues of these less fortunate members. This practice was dropped in 1981-1982 in accordance with the ruling by the IRS in that period (see Chapter 7).

In later years, however, a so-called Almoner (one who distributes alms) Fund was established out of which such dues could be paid. And more recently, the Gregory Trust was created by a bequest from former Club Member W. A. Gregory for a similar purpose.

The Club has also been the grateful recipient of grants from time to time from the Edyth Bush Charitable Foundation. The Foundation contributed generously to a major building project and the Financial Luncheon program.

Throughout the history of the Club many appeals have been made for donations and members have always responded generously, especially for building improvements. The following have contributed amounts above $10,000: Raymond C. Baker, Lorene Banta (in memory of her husband Cornelius), M. Elizabeth Brothers, Deloris Burke, Genevieve (Vee) Florea (in memory of her parents Earl and Eunice Taylor), Arthur Normandin, and Carolyn Shinkle.

Gifts in the range of $5,000 to $9,999 have been received from Opal Benson, Bob Copeland (in memory of his wife Murrell), Betty Dunn, Frank C. Linn, Raymond and Isobel Mancha, Bill and Joyce Munsie, Kenneth W. Osborne, Edward Robinson, Ralph and Barbara Rogers, Nicholas Schmidt, Dick Sewell, and Ann MacArthur Sherman. Many others have contributed smaller amounts year after year.

With the aging of the building it became clear that funds were continually needed for major maintenance and equipment replacement, requiring repeated requests for member donations. They have always responded generously. To avoid these special requests and encourage donations for other purposes, a Major Maintenance reserve fund was created in 2000 with noncash transfers of funds from the operating account based on the life of items such as the roof, roads, painting, air-conditioning, and other elements requiring maintenance and replacement. This fund has grown to some $170,000 and is sufficient to cover most foreseeable major maintenance issues and replacement costs.

Investments

Oversight of the finances is in the hands of the Vice President of Finance, the Treasurer, and the Assistant Treasurer. The Finance Vice President chairs a committee composed of six members, each appointed for staggered three-year terms to provide continuity.

The Club is fortunate to have available highly qualified experts in the fields of investments, banking, economics, non-profit investing, and accounting. The Committee reports to the Board at least monthly.

A detailed conservative investment policy was established and approved by the Board in the year 2000 and has continued to be used with minor amendments. The policy has served the Club well. All monies are managed in an investment pool and withdrawals are made from each fund in accordance with the required restrictions. Withdrawals are based on five percent of the three-year moving average of the market value of the investment pool.

Vice Presidents of Finance Bill Williams and Clayton Swain have made major contributions to the Club, serving successively as Chairs of this committee. Their diligence throughout the recurring ups and downs of the market have kept the Club's investments on track, contributing to the overall stability of the Club.

As the Club grew it became necessary to do an annual audit of the finances and for many years a qualified member, Weldon Manwaring, served in this capacity followed by Member Tom Poole and others. When more money became involved, the Club was advised to use an outside auditor to conduct a review of the accounts and prepare the annual report to the IRS. This was accomplished in 2000, when CPA Edward Langdon was hired to serve as Auditor.

Rentals

To help defray the expenses of operating the Club, the premises are occasionally rented. Members pay a minimum fee plus direct expenses for hosting weddings, anniversaries, memorials, and similar personal events at the Club. As a part of the mission to contribute to the community, only minimum out-of-pocket costs are charged for nonprofit organizations such as Rollins College, the University of Central Florida, the English-Speaking Union, and many others. Some of these organizations make voluntary contributions to the Club.

The Club is also available to members of the public, especially for wedding receptions. These rentals are an important source of revenue for the Club.

The Club has been the recipient of many gifts, donations, and bequests over the years. The generosity of the members is a tribute to their love of the organization.

CHAPTER 9

The Club and the Community

The early relationship with the Chamber of Commerce was vital to the early existence of the Club, and the connection has remained a strong one throughout the succeeding years. The independence of the Club was soon established, but many members of the Club have been Board members of the Chamber, and the relationship has remained a cordial one.

Education

The early connection with Rollins College has been continuously important to both the Club and the college. Every Rollins president since 1934 — when Dr. Hamilton Holt was a founding member of the Club — has held membership in the University Club. And so have many of the Rollins faculty and staff.

The earliest scholarships granted by the Club were from a gift of $40,000 by R. T. Miller, a longtime benefactor and repeated "anonymous donor" to the Club. This sum was later increased by $10,000 from Mr. Miller. This gift was directed to be administered by a committee of the University Club, and the amount drawn from the fund in payment of scholarships was to be matched by the College. In his book, *The First Twenty-five Years of the University Club of Winter Park*, William Stark (President 1956-1957) wrote,

The fund set up by Mr. Miller will soon be completely expended. It has furthered the education of twenty-eight promising students... Query: might the Club consider the possibility of replenishing the fund and continuing the service?

Stark also wrote that in the Charter of the Club, originally approved in April of 1937, the object of the Club included the aid and financial assistance of worthy students while seeking an education.

In the succeeding several years, various proposals were made for implementing this purpose, but it was not until 1943 that a plan was adopted for a Student Aid Fund, which would be administered by six trustees. For some years this fund was supported by voluntary contributions from members.

In 1965, the Education Assistance Committee was formed to make recommendations on scholarship awards with the Board making the final decisions. The Education Assistance Fund had steadily grown through members' donations and bequests, amounting to more than $125,000 in 1994. By 2010, it had grown to $180,000.

For many years, awards were given only to students of Rollins College but after the creation of the University of Central Florida (originally Florida Technological University), scholarships were also awarded to that institution. The recipients are honored at a regular Club dinner ("Rollins Night" or "UCF Night") at which the President of the institution or another high-ranking administrative officer accepts the award.

The Board honored Bob Wilkinson (President 1980-1981) in 2008 with the naming of the award to the University of Central Florida, the Robert F. Wilkinson Scholarship Award, in recognition of his long and faithful service. In the same year, the award to Rollins College was named the M. Elizabeth Brothers Scholarship Award, in honor of the first woman to join and the first President of the Club.

Scholarship aid has been offered more recently to Valencia Community College and Seminole State College (formerly

Seminole Community College). Presentations are made at a Club dinner.

Community Grants

Another community activity of the Club is administered through the Community Assistance Committee. The Fund is largely used to benefit the community of Winter Park, which in 2010 had a population of some 28,000. From early years, the Club directed assistance to the neighborhood on the west side of Winter Park.

The Winter Park Community Center on West New England Avenue was founded with substantial help from the Club. Later assistance went to the DePugh Nursing Home (which is the first such facility established for African-Americans in the state), the Welbourne Avenue Nursery and Day Care Center, Meals on Wheels, and others.

In more recent years, grants were given to Harbor House, Christian Service Center, Lighthouse of Central Florida, Winter Park Day Nursery, Negro Spiritual Scholarship Foundation, VoTech Student Emergency Fund, The Sharing Center, and Pathways to Care, among other local nonprofit organizations.

Other Outreach

The popular weekly Financial Luncheons mentioned earlier were a cooperative effort among the Club, Rollins College, the Edyth Bush Charitable Foundation, the Morse Museum of American Art, and the Winter Park Library. The Winter Park Chamber of Commerce was added in 2007. These luncheons began some years previously, meeting from September through May during the winter months at two popular restaurants in Winter Park, and as noted earlier, the meeting location was changed to the University Club in 1981. These were catered luncheons, with a speaker who was an expert in some aspect of finance; they were open to the public. In light of diminishing attendance, the Financial Luncheon Group was discontinued in April 2008 and a series of breakfast meetings was substituted, beginning on September 18, 2008. Unfortunately, the attendance was not sufficient to support them and the last breakfast meeting was held in April 2009.

The Clubhouse is made available to several nonprofit organizations on a regular basis for their meetings. The local branch of the English-Speaking Union has used the Club facilities for many years and the Asia Society holds all of its regular meetings there. In addition, the American Association of Individual Investors (AAII) holds a monthly meeting at the University Club (in the evenings) from September through May. AAII members as well as nonmembers may attend for a nominal charge. The program consists of a speaker who covers a variety of financial subjects.

Other local organizations that have used the Club facilities include the Harvard Alumni Club, the Wellesley and Smith Alumnae Clubs, and the American Association of University Women. The Trinity Preparatory School, League of Women Voters, Club Holland, Spellbinders, and several Rotary Clubs have all met at the Club.

In addition, the Clubhouse is available for groups to present topics of general community concern, and the Club has sponsored lectures, debates, and concerts, open to the public.

Many members of the Club are individually active in numerous volunteer community organizations—Meals on Wheels, for instance—giving countless hours of public and community service.

Several Club members have been elected officials of Winter Park. Others have been state and federal legislators. Club members now serve as volunteers in museums, libraries, hospitals, and historical sites in the city. They welcome opportunities for community involvement, and make a special effort to increase public awareness of the Club among residents of Winter Park and the surrounding area.

The Club's web site (created in 2007) has been helpful in presenting detailed information about the Club to members and prospective members. Monthly editions of the *Club Times* are regularly featured, along with any special events, including those open to the public.

The Club has a long tradition of serving the surrounding community and in recent years has placed increased emphasis on that aspect of its goals, objectives, and purpose. It continues to be a vital part of the culture and community of Winter Park.

CHAPTER 10

Meetings and Programs

A s is well-known,, the Club was formed in March of 1934 with twenty-eight members, but no organization and formal planning took place until January of 1935. The winter residents, who made up the bulk of the membership, were then back in town and ready to proceed with the new organization.

Most of the members were retirees, a large portion of them academics. Many were men of national distinction, eager to share their knowledge and experiences with others of a similar background. The few full-time resident members of Winter Park were mostly Rollins staff or faculty, with a sprinkling of men of other professions.

After the first year, the meetings consisted of biweekly Saturday evening dinners at a restaurant, then a move to another place (first the Chamber of Commerce, later the borrowed room at the Country Club, then the Little Harris Clubhouse), with group singing following the dinner and preceding the lecture.

The lectures were usually given by one of the members, with lively discussions following the presentation. These were scholarly talks, and after a few years they began to be digested and analyzed by the Secretary and preserved in the minutes. The minutes of those meetings indicate the serious nature of the Club.

For the lectures were determinedly academic. An anecdotal report says that one such talk was supposedly titled "The Mating Rituals of the Tse-Tse Fly in Guatemala in 1910."

And the early discussions seem to have been equally serious. But one (certainly apocryphal) incident has it that a guest (and potential member) fled because the members were telling jokes in Latin.

The Powwows began in 1938, and afternoon meetings were limited strictly to one hour. These were held on Friday afternoons in the beginning, but proved so popular that two sessions, one on Tuesdays, were soon scheduled, with the idea that members would attend one or the other. The crowding of the small quarters was not relieved, however, because nearly all the members attended both programs.

The Powwows had begun because it was found that members would gather into lively conversation groups before and after the dinner meetings, and it seemed that a seminar-type meeting would be popular. It was.

One early meeting consisted of a program presented by Madam Louise Homer, the great contralto of the Metropolitan Opera Company, who had retired to Winter Park with her husband, Sidney Homer, a famous musicologist of the time and a member of the Club. (No other program given by a woman is mentioned in the minutes for many years.)

The Saturday evening dinners lasted throughout the season, usually November through April, then ceased for the other six months. Customarily the dinners were men-only affairs, though reference is made in the minutes to the fact that an "annual ladies' night" was held. Interestingly, some were not dinners, but evening occasions, with refreshments being served after the program. At least one of the men-only dinner meetings fell on New Year's Eve. One can only speculate on the reaction of some of the wives.

The minutes occasionally mention discussions about inviting the ladies to one or another of the meetings. Frequently these suggestions were voted down. One discussion was about the appropriateness of inviting the ladies to dinner to hear a talk being given by Dr. Marie Dye, Nutritionist, on proper diet for the older person. And at least one of the ladies' nights hosted by the Club was held at the Woman's Club of Winter Park.

Another meeting in the early years was publicized to the membership by means of a penny postcard that read

> The next meeting of the Club will be held in the Chamber of Commerce Building at 8 o'clock on Saturday evening April 11. Dr. Richard Burton will speak on "Startling Revelations Concerning Mark Twain." As this is the last night of the season, we are making it Ladies' Night. The usual supper will be omitted.

When the Club was formed, the idea of anything other than an organization of college-educated, white men never entered the mind of anyone concerned — nor did any such notion occur to the members, apparently, for many years.

The organization was originally thought of as a club for retirees, and nearly all the members were. They took great satisfaction, justly so, in their own accomplishments and knowledge and in those of their colleagues.

If there was a hint of prideful self-satisfaction in their attitude, there was a reason for it. The number of those claimed to be listed in *Who's Who in America* (fifty-nine in the early years) was astonishing for a town the size of Winter Park (see Appendix A). Their concentration in one new organization was even more amazing.

The Club was described as providing an "intellectual feast," and reviews of the lectures would grant this to be so. It was also referred to as an "intellectual spa," a "gathering of great minds," an "Athens of the South." Perhaps the phrasing was a bit overblown. Nevertheless, the Club was a truly unique organization.

There were other university clubs in the country (including one in downtown Orlando), but none with the purposes of this one. This was a unique club where ideas were explored and challenged. This was also a club that saw itself as an educational and charitable organization.

Very early the new club made plain that it did not wish to be a university club like others so common in other cities. There was to be no "networking," that is, business referrals within the group. There was to be no using Club mailing lists for prospecting.

There was to be no private business transacted at any Club gatherings. No one should promote their business or services. These were gentlemen's agreements.

Ideally, titles and honorifics were not to be used, though in the records "Dr." and "Gen." and "Col." do often appear. But clearly the egalitarian ideal among the members was strong.

The fact that the Club was predominantly an association of retirees ensured losses every year, which were made up by the entrance of new, usually younger, members. Wrote William Stark (President 1956-1957):

> For one who has known the Club for many years, this rather steady shifting of the membership has been extremely valuable. The Club's success is dependent upon the leadership of its outstanding members as speakers, as executives, as experts in various fields including human relations. In twenty-five years, among the more than 2,000 men who have belonged to the Club, many notable figures have helped to make the organization tick and to make it an inspiration to their fellow members. Most of the leaders of the earlier years are gone or have become less active, but these others are always able and willing to take over the responsibilities and satisfactions of carrying on.

What may be described as normal attrition usually reduced the yearly membership. Thus, the net gain amounted to only sixty-six in the five years 1954-1959.

Wrote William Stark again in 1959:

We are rather proud of our maturity. We have more members still active in their vocations than we had in the earlier years of the Club, but three-fourths of the members continue to be more than sixty years of age. Studies of age distribution in 1947, 1952, and 1959 agree in placing the median age between 70 and 72, and the lower limit of the oldest fourth at 77. On July 20, 1959, seventeen members had passed their 90th birthday, the oldest being in the second half of his 98th year.

Interestingly, though the early members were older men, there was a tinge of what today we would call "ageism" among some. One retiring president (Wesley Frost) wrote in 1959, "The ideal age for the principal officers is in the range from 67 to 72. Older men are under strain, younger men less sapient in the concerns affecting the Club."

Over the years the members have reflected the time and place in which they lived. All the founding members (except Carter Bradford, who was involved in the founding because his job with the Chamber of Commerce) were born in the latter half of the nineteenth century. They were Victorians in the literal sense of the term. Even young (age 28) Bradford missed the Victorian era by only four years.

They were comfortable professional men, mostly retirees, well-intentioned, conservative. Nearly all had lived in the North, where few African-Americans then lived; most had attended all-male, all-white colleges and universities (except for several Oberlin alumni and a few others from nonsegregated and coeducational institutions). They were in a rigorously segregated community. But they did have in Rollins the example of a coeducational college.

For the most part, their view of "ladies" was respectful, paternalistic, and somewhat condescending. In the very early years, Dr. George Whicher had expressed the view that it was very good for the "ladies" to have their own clubs so that they could learn organizational skills and pursue their own interests. And Wesley Frost (President 1958-1959) spoke of the appropriate ages for service to the Club saying that "The Club should be kept strictly a men's club, as per first-President Whicher's wise thought—"It does the ladies good to find themselves organizing and operating their clubs and groups."

Gradually, however, women were invited to more and more of the meetings—always as guests and with no thought by anyone that a "lady," however well-educated, might be considered for membership. Eventually the Tuesday afternoon Powwows became open to women visitors. By the 1970s it was customary for the wives of the members to attend the dinners—in long gowns.

Wives were "invited" to make sandwiches when the occasion required, and to arrange flowers for the dinner tables. The Friday Powwows were never open to the "ladies" because that was the regular meeting-day of the Woman's Club of Winter Park. As Virgil Hartsock (President 1981-1982) remembers, there was always a rush to get the Friday meeting over promptly at 4:00 o'clock so that the "ladies" could be picked up following their meeting and tea.

In 1966, Mary Dublin Keyserling spoke to a Powwow. She was the head of the Women's Bureau of the United States Department of Labor and at that time the highest-ranking woman in the Federal government, wife of Leon Keyserling, sometime-chief of the President's economic advisers. Her father was Dr. Louis I. Dublin, world-famous authority on public health, and a member of the Club.

The records indicate that the second woman to address a dinner meeting was Alice Suffield (later Britton), who was the daughter of Dr. Lester O. Schriver (President 1970-1972). To have a woman address a dinner meeting was sufficiently startling that the *Orlando Sentinel*, in speaking of the event, headlined on September 23, 1970, "Has Women's Lib Come to the University Club?"

When the Tuesday Powwows were discontinued because of declining attendance, the women were allowed to attend the Friday meetings. The Woman's Club soon changed its meeting day to Thursday, because so many members chose to attend the University Club sessions.

With the further decline in attendance at the Friday afternoon meetings, a series of lunches with speakers was initiated. They have been somewhat successful.

The biweekly dinners were held for many years on Saturday evenings, except in the summer months when they were held on Fridays. This seemed an increasingly puzzling arrangement, and the dinners were eventually shifted to Fridays all year around. This is the schedule, with a few exceptions, in 2010.

By the mid-1970s the minutes indicate that there were occasional murmurings about opening the membership to women. The ruling of the IRS (see Chapter 7) removed any ambiguity. Elizabeth Brothers of Rollins College became the first woman member of the University Club in 1981 (and later, in 1999, the first female President). In 1982, nine women joined and in the succeeding years, many more. In 2010 forty-eight percent of the total membership consisted of women.

This was not an easy transition. There was vigorous and vocal opposition by some of the members—and, curiously enough, by some of their wives. The firm IRS position was that tax exemption could not be granted in the face of obvious discrimination. In the years that have passed, the active participation of women has become an accepted and welcome thing—even in the Men's Chorus, now titled the University Club Chorus. The duplicate bridge group, long a determinedly male activity, eventually accepted women players, and has numbered several among its regular members.

The Club and its meetings and programs began to gradually change in the late 1980s. Daytime meetings of specific interest groups became more popular. (A list of the Intellectual Activity groups active in 2010 is listed in Chapter 11.)

The Friday dinners and lunches at the Club also began changing in the late 1990s and early 2000s in answer to the members' requests. Instead of lectures, the Program Committee scheduled more general cultural programs on Friday nights. These concerts and presentations proved popular and the appearance of opera, ballet, jazz groups, and string quartets along with other performing artists, enhanced the Club cultural experience. Lectures were also included in the mix. Some twenty-four dinners were booked in 2010.

Many of the Friday evening dinners sold out to the capacity of 152 members and guests—and had waiting lists. And the dinners became a recruitment tool for new members. After many years of experience the Program Committee determined that any dinner or luncheon program should last no longer than forty-five minutes. This was deemed to be about the attention span of the members after a full meal. It became a tradition that questions and answers could be part of the lectures at the luncheons, but not after dinners.

Attendance at the Friday lunches, however, continued to decline during the same period with attendance often fewer than sixty members and guests. The six to nine lunches each year largely featured lectures. A few members objected to the program changes at the dinners, preferring more substantial fare in the form of lectures, at both dinners and lunches.

The Program Committee also scheduled many special events for the members including Super Bowl watch parties and a traditional New Year's Day dance and reception. Periodic field trips to nearby attractions also proved somewhat popular. In addition, the Membership Committee sponsored a few special events (including a Kentucky Derby party) and the Development Committee conducted fund-raisers. All of the lunches, dinners, and special events are self-supporting.

In 2006, the Club also began the popular "After Hours" event. The Friday evening dinner programs were concluded by 8:30 p.m. Noting that many members adjourned to nearby restaurants/bars for more social intercourse, the Club Library was turned into an intimate cabaret-type setting, complete with a piano singalong by members and guests. Thus the tradition of songs after dinner from the early days of the Club was honored. The members and their guests enjoyed after-dinner liqueurs, coffee, and chocolate. For many years, venerable Club member Victor Tipton played the piano.

It also became the practice of the Membership Committee to hold special meetings to induct new members. In 2010 these took place three times a year, or whenever there was a sufficiently large group of inductees.

The meetings usually occur on a Friday afternoon. Each new member is photographed individually for the "Rogues' Gallery," a photo album that contains the pictures, together with the names and dates. This family album is kept in the library for perusal by the members. This is followed by a program of orientation. At that time they are introduced to a visual history of the Club and to its present activities.

Following the picture-taking and orientation, the meeting is open to the entire membership. At that time, the new members become the program. Each new member gives a short speech outlining his or her background and area of expertise. After these get-acquainted speeches, the new and old members mingle for conversation and refreshments.

The meetings and interests of the members have changed over the years, responding to the times and desires of the membership. The leadership of the Club continues to adapt to their interests and pursuits.

CHAPTER 11

Intellectual and Cultural Activities

In 2010, the Club continued to adhere to its purpose, Charter, and Bylaws. This effort encompassed and manifested itself in its attention to the visual arts, the Library, and the vitality of Intellectual Activities.

Interest groups flourished in the Club almost from its inception. As previously noted, they were an outgrowth of the Powwows, which themselves grew out of the interest of the members in listening to lectures and then engaging in free discussion on a given subject. As previously mentioned, the very first of such groups was the coterie of avid bridge players who eagerly assembled following the Powwows, expressing irritation if the discussion lasted beyond 4:00 p.m.

In 2009-10 there were three Bridge Groups — two Duplicate and one Social — which meet weekly. A Bridge Class was also introduced that year.

Other activities over the years have included conversation and instruction in Spanish, French, and German. These classes have been led by experts in their particular field and enjoyed by many participants.

The Book Review Group, originally called the Round Table, was one of the early activities and its popularity continued to draw good audiences in 2010. In 1958 the group listed the following as requirement for its members:

1. review a book of the member's own choosing;
2. attend regularly; and
3. lead a discussion.

Some fifty years later, the rules of this group had been somewhat relaxed. Often the discussion is omitted entirely and the review takes up most of the allotted hour, followed by questions and answers from the attendees.

The Club and its intellectual meetings began to gradually change in the late 1980s. Daytime meetings of specific interest groups became very popular. The smaller gatherings focused on singular topic areas of interest to particular members.

While many of the groups had been in existence for some time, their growth was recognized and formalized by Dan Schulz (President 2004-2006) and the Board with the creation of a Vice President of Intellectual Activities position. Calling these groups the "Soul of the Club," Schulz began a concerted effort to emphasize them, which was continued by subsequent Presidents.

In 2010, under the able leadership of Vice Presidents Dot Cline and Florence Bacas Snow, there were some thirty-five such groups meeting periodically in the Club, mostly in the daytime hours.

The small assemblages change periodically according to the interests of the members. Some are longstanding and others are created with Board approval or dropped because of diminishing interest.

In the decade preceding the publication of this book, many activities were introduced and some continue to the present. The Current Events Group has been popular for many years and continually enjoys a large and enthusiastic attendance. The weekly discussions have drawn the largest number of members. Often as many as sixty attendees have discussed and debated current events. In 2010 another group with an equal number of members gathered to attend the new Classical Music activity, led by Joe Rizzo (President 2006-2007) and Member George Gascon, with their extensive knowledge of — and contacts with — the local classical music community.

An Intellectual Activities Gathering

Other weekly activities that year were the History Group, which had many avid attendees, and groups such as Genealogy, Science, Computer Users, Health and Wellness, and Loss Support were attended by fellow members interested in pursuing in-depth knowledge in specific areas.

The Club continues to encourage its members to offer new ideas for new activities. Several new intellectual activities were formed in 2009-10, including Book Reading and Legacy Writing, but most notable was the addition of some evening programs. As members of our society reach retirement age, the Club offered activities that were less structured, thus providing members, their guests, and the public an informal setting for interaction in various intellectually stimulating activities. Some of those evening activities in 2010 included Opera Appreciation, Film Group, Trivia4U, Current Events Evening, and Open Mike. The evening activities were planned to attract members and nonmembers who worked during the daytime hours. Another evening activity, the Debate Series, presented professionals versed in particular areas of knowledge, debating important current issues. The series was attractive to members of the public.

Many groups have sprung up over the years and flourished for a time, but then disappeared. The Camera Group, for instance, had many enthusiastic members for some years. It was said that, eventually, the discussions became so technical that many of the amateur camera buffs felt intimidated. The Club tradition of showing travelogues at some of the dinner meetings grew into the Travel Group but that, too, was no longer offered in the 21st century. In 1963 a Golf Group was formed but it has long since disappeared.

For some time there was an active Garden Group. At least one elaborate Rose Show was organized and held at the Clubhouse, filling the Auditorium with arrangements and fine specimens. The Garden Group later became known as the Garden and Hobby Group, then disappeared.

A Drama Group existed for a time, followed sometime later by the current Play Reading Group. A Women's Chorus and an Orchestra Group, once popular, were also discontinued.

The Men's Chorus, however, flourished for many years and continued its enthusiastic activity in 2009-10. This group met regularly, practiced faithfully, and presented two concerts a year at Christmas and in the spring. The group grew out of a "Boys Choir" from an earlier time, which was the outgrowth of the male quartets and singalongs after dinners in the early days of the Club. The Men's Chorus was renamed the University Club Chorus in 2010, and now includes women.

Boys' Choir circa 1950-60

Men's Chorus 2007-08

The Philosophical Discussion Group, headed for many years by long-time Member Peggy Kraemer, has met weekly for years and attracts a good audience. There is usually a lecture program followed by discussion. Frequently, the lecturer is a Rollins or UCF professor, but often the leader is a Club member knowledgeable in the subject discussed. The History Group has also enjoyed great periods of popularity.

Special Programs offered by the Club sometimes become partnering programs, joining with local area organizations such as the Winter Park Library (for example, Spellbinders and Brain Health), the Florida Writers Association (Florida Writers Group), and the Central Florida Genealogical Society (Genealogy Group). They focus on specific subject matters. These groups meet monthly and are headed by Club members and the local-area organizations. They are attended by members of the Club and of the specific organization, as well as the public.

All of the Intellectual Activities are open to the public, as part of the Club's ongoing efforts to better serve the community. The Intellectual Activities groups are the soul of the Club. They provide intellectual stimulation, camaraderie, and social intercourse for the Club's members and the public-at-large. In 2010 the following groups were active.

Daytime

Book Readers
Book Review
Bridge–Duplicate
Bridge–Open
Classical Music Group
Computer Users
Craft Group
Current Events
French, Conversational
Genealogy
Health and Wellness
History Group
Loss Support
Medical Forum
Men's Chorus
Philosophical Discussion
Play Reading
Science Group
Stock Market Analysis

Evening

Current Events
Debate Series
Film Group
Florida Writers
Open Mike–Poetry
Opera Appreciation
Trivia4U
Legacy Writing

Morning Classes

German, Beginners
German, Conversational
Spanish, Conversational
Spanish, Beg/Inter
Bridge Class

Library

To aid in the studies undertaken by many of the Intellectual Activity groups and also by individual members, the Club maintains a much-appreciated Library. Since its early creation, the Library has been a source of pride and pleasure for the members.

The first mention of the Library occurs in the minutes of the regular meeting of January 15, 1938, when Dr. Octavius Applegate, Librarian, reported the possession of ten autographed volumes and thirteen other books given by members. Three months later, the number of autographed books had increased to forty-six. Books and magazines were placed in the Little Harris Clubhouse in a small bookcase, which had been made by some of the members to fit odd wall spaces. William Stark (President 1956-1957 and Historian) commented as follows.

> An anonymous donor offered to match gifts to a library fund up to a total of $2,500 at the beginning of the next Club year. An allotment of $500 was made from the Club treasury.

In the early years, the Club was fortunate in having in its membership a noted professional librarian, who directed the organization of the new library and the selection of standard reference books. Management of the library was in the hands of the Library Committee, with its Chair reporting to the President.

When the Club moved to the new quarters in 1948, a small room behind the auditorium was specifically designed for the Library. This room became the Reading Room when the larger Library was added; the Fiction and Biography sections are shelved there. Between 1938 and 1948, the collection expanded from donations and Club operating funds, but despite rapid membership growth, members feared they might never be able to fill all the shelves in that new room. By the 1970s, however, the collection overflowed the small area and the Committee had to begin, reluctantly, deaccessioning rarely used materials.

After many years of discussion, the Library addition in 1986-87 solved the problem of the overflow (see Chapter 4). Club members now find serious nonfiction and fiction books there for reference and recreational reading. The Library subscribes to some periodicals, and members donate more from private subscriptions and are also generous with donations of books.

The Library also serves as a meeting room for committees and many of the activity groups, and also as a reception area before Friday night dinners and a cabaret room later in the evenings for the popular After Hours gatherings.

Over the years, furniture has been added to the room: two large wooden tables, six chairs in antiqued gold vinyl, a globe stand, a dictionary stand, a step-stool, a freestanding wooden bookcase for the Great Books series, two book carts, a file cabinet, three display stands, and a wooden card catalogue.

The Library Committee, under the direction of Martha Williamson and Dana Schmidt, meets weekly for work sessions. At one time, James Bryan, Past President of the American Library Association, was a member of that committee.

Since 2005, the committee has been updating the Library. Drawing on its rich resources, the Club is grateful to have had professional librarians and other members with varied skills who are needed to maintain an active library. The inventory stood at about 4,000 titles in 2010.

The Library also contains a unique collection of books by its members. The "ten autographed volumes" from 1938 framed the start of the author-member section. Author Ray Stannard Baker was active during his years with the Club. Joseph C. Daniels was the author of many popular novels. William Hazlett Upson, author of the "Earthworm Tractor" stories popular for many years in *The Saturday Evening Post* was a member. Paul R. Alley joined the Club in 1984; he was the writer, producer, and narrator of the first nightly newscast aired on NBC television. Dr. Mark Skousen, nationally known financial writer, joined in 1986.

In more recent years, Doug Waitley, author of many books about Florida, is a valued member, as is Bob Reed (President 1907-1908), author of three nonfiction and four fiction books. Current Member Gerry Schiffhorst has published nine books, and Betty Hill is the author of many children's books. Member Dean Warren has also written several books, many of them of the sci-fi genre. A section of books by Club members is featured in the Library. It contains 306 books.

The Library continues to grow more popular with members, and after seventy-two years, it is well on its way to serving the members in accordance with Article 3.1 of the Club's Charter.

Art Gallery

After the move into the new building in 1948, a desire arose among the Club's members that some art works should be displayed on its walls. By the early 1970s, a vigorous Art Committee was formed and exhibitions of various members' works were tentatively scheduled from time to time. These shows were open only to the membership and were held on Sunday afternoons.

In more recent years the exhibits have become a valued feature of the Club's activities and they were opened to the public in the 1990s. The shows are no longer confined to the works of members, although members' art works are still occasionally on display.

A different local artist is featured every month (at no commission and no cost to the artist) and follows the tradition of a Sunday afternoon reception, with refreshments provided by the host artist. Since 2005, the art works have been coordinated and displayed under the supervision of Gallery Arts Chair Nita Marie Rizzo, assisted by Members Daphne Frutchey and George Stewart. As the 75th Anniversary year was winding down, some sixty local artists had exhibited at the Club, and the Gallery was booked for the following fifteen months.

The Art Gallery

The Club's focus on Art, the Library, and most particularly on the many Intellectual Activities groups, is in keeping with its purposes. New groups form and old groups dissolve, according to the interests of the members. It is truly as the Club motto asserts: *Intellectio Sodalitas* – Fellowship in Knowledge and Understanding.

PART III

CHAPTER 12

The Members

The professional diversity among the Club members over the years has led to the education of one another. For the members come from a variety of backgrounds.

There are two major sources for information about the professions of members of the Club—the application for membership forms and the annual *Yearbook*. The *Yearbooks* date back to 1935-36. They contain member names, degrees, year of joining, sorority/fraternity membership, phone number, address, and profession. The information is provided by the members themselves.

As discussed previously, in the early years academics and clergymen formed a large proportion of the membership, with a sprinkling of bankers, other businessmen, and professionals. Later membership was broadened to include members from all walks of life.

By 2010, the professional makeup of the Club's membership had changed in accordance with societal changes and was more varied and complex than in previous years. According to the *Yearbook* that year, members with careers in business and banking represented about eighteen percent of the membership while education careers represented nineteen percent. Members involved in medical/dental/nursing professions amounted to seven percent and the professions of engineering and law were seven and six percent, respectively. The remaining fifty percent of the membership were involved in or had pursued careers in music, art, writing, diplomatic service, real estate, military, computer science, and other professions.

The overall image of the members during its 75-year history, however is, that of a community of educated professionals. Most are retired.

A study in 2003 under the leadership of Fred Rosenthal (President 2003-2004) reported that about half of the members received their degrees by 1950. Many of these degrees were post-WW II efforts. They used the GI Bill. Some fifteen percent received their degrees during the war, and thirteen percent had completed degree work before the war.

Wives' names were published opposite the husbands' name for the first time in the 1981-1982 *Yearbook* during the presidency of Virgil Hartsock. After women were admitted to membership that year, a "spouse" name was listed beside the member's name, along with her professional career or interest. Since then, there has been a steady increase in women's membership. In 2010, forty-eight percent of the Club membership were women.

Year-End Membership

1970	1980	1990	2000	2010
862	695	725	704	460

The membership peaked in 1961 at 950, decreased somewhat, but then held steady at about 700 for many years. A loss of male membership beginning in 1981 was offset by the influx of women, as they became eligible for membership. However, the organization was becoming short of the number needed to financially support itself. The decline in membership as recorded in the Club archives has been most noticeable in the first decade of the twenty-first century. The Club lost 244 members during that period.

By the end of 2003, the declining membership was a recurrent problem, as reflected in the minutes of the Board. In an effort to gain some perspective on the membership problem and the future of the Club, Fred Rosenthal (President 2003-2004) convened an all-day meeting of the Board in November of 2003 to establish some long-range planning. The retreat examined the Club's attributes and delineated its detriments and problems. The resulting profile of the Club continues to be an important account of the Club's status in this new century.

Using Rosenthal's study and with new documents, Bob Reed (President 2007-2008) convened another all-day retreat of the Board and the Presidents Emeriti at Rollins College in the summer of 2007. The declining membership was the central issue of concern.

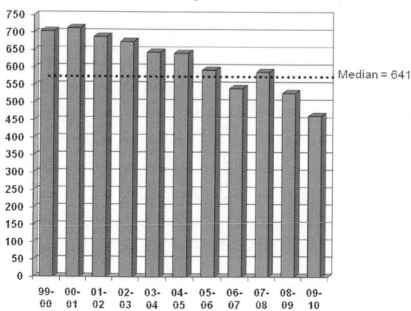

End-of-Year Membership Numbers, 1999 to 2010, by Fiscal Year

An analysis by Sharon Knapp (Vice President Membership) in 2009-2010 illustrated the problem faced by the Club in the past few years. Membership dropped in almost every year from 1999 to 2010. The only increases were in 2000 and 2007. The median membership in that decade was 641.

New member recruitment became a priority of every president during those years. A number of strategies were tried to attract new members, most successfully the 90-Day-Campaign in the fall of 2007 under the leadership of Bob Reed (President 2007-2008) and Ken Rugh (Vice President Membership). That concentrated campaign brought in ninety-eight new members, the most in recent years.

The number of members at the end of 2009-2010 was 460. The chart below shows the *net* gain/loss of members in the first decade of the 21st century. Median member annual loss during that period was twenty-eight.

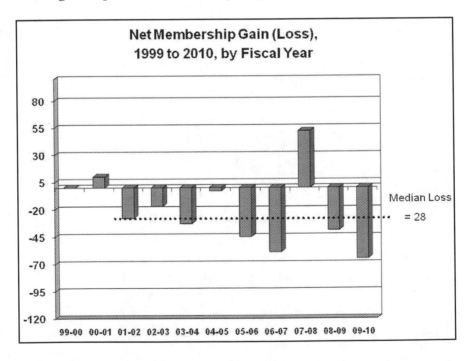

A number of activities to attract the public (and possible members) to the Club have been mounted in recent years.

Open Houses, Wine Tastings, Outdoor Band Concerts, MusicFests, and ArtFests on the Lawn have been held. Evening dance lessons and trivia quizzes — open to the public — have also been scheduled.

The most successful recruiting tactic over the years, however, has proved to be word of mouth — members recommending the Club to friends, bringing them as guests, and serving as sponsors for full membership.

This chart describes the characteristics of Club membership as determined by the 2009-2010 Sharon Knapp study.

Age at joining	68 years (range 26-89)
Current age	77 years (range 37-103)
Years of membership	6.7 years

A basic problem in membership has been the retention of new members. Under the leadership of Dan Schulz (President 2004-2006), the Amigo Committee was created, dedicated to making new members welcome, nurturing their membership, and encouraging active participation in Club activities. In 2010, a Fellowship Committee was created with similar goals.

Still, membership retention and decline remains a continuing problem as the Club advances into the twenty-first century. As Max Reed (President 2009-2010) noted in her inaugural speech, the focus of the modern Club must be on the Three Rs of Membership: Recruitment, Retention, and Replacement. During the years 2009-2010, the Board voted to implement a rarely used Bylaw that gave the option of a lifetime membership and the elimination of any dues for a member who reached the age of 100. Several members availed themselves of the lifetime opportunity; only one or two were eligible for no dues.

As previously stated, nearly all of the initial members of the Club were temporary winter residents with their permanent homes elsewhere. Most of the members gave two addresses—Winter Park and "home." Within only a few years, a shift could be detected. Increasingly, only one address was listed. Only a handful of members gives two addresses in 2010, with most spending most of the year in Winter Park or nearby communities.

So most of the members now call Winter Park home. With this has come a greater involvement of the members in other organizations in the community and the civic life of the community. (see Chapter 9.)

In the early years the membership dues were low and the expenses were negligible. It was the policy for many years to keep the dues at a minimum, and to count on gifts from members to balance the budget. As recently as 1975 the dues were $25 and the membership a comfortable 869.

Dues Increases, 1994-2009:

1994-95	$155	2002-03	$185
1995-96	$165	2003-04	$200
1996-97	$165	2004-05	$275
1997-98	$175	2005-06	$275
1998-99	$150	2006-07	$275
1999-00	$165	2007-08	$275
2000-01	$170	2008-09	$275
2001-02	$180	2009-10	$300

Beginning in 1994, the dues were held stable or raised only slightly, making it difficult to achieve financial stability. The prevailing feeling was that any raise in dues resulted in a loss of membership. But the dues were not sufficiently increased in the new century to support the operation of the Club.

Under the leadership of Richard Artz (President 1998-1999) and later Dan Schulz (President 2004-2006), an emphasis on spousal membership (at a reduced price) was undertaken. The Club had ninety-two spouse members in 2010.

As noted, in the early years there was an expressed feeling of sentiment and even boyish camaraderie by the male members. There was the Club song, sung after dinners. It was sentimental and evocative of college days. It provokes smiles now, yet it reflects the nostalgia felt in earlier days and is part of what the Club is now.

The deep feeling of many for the Club is reflected in the fact that many members have celebrated significant events, such as anniversaries, at the Clubhouse, and memorial services for several members and/or their spouses have been conducted in the Auditorium.

The University Club remains an organization of men and women of whatever race or creed who are bound by a comity of interest in things of the mind and a concern for the wider community. The Club has not seriously altered its basic purpose since 1934, though there have been changes as the times and culture have changed. The founders' emphasis on scholarly activity and interests has evolved to a broader, more inclusive posture. The changes have been in answer to the majority of members' desires.

And the great distinction of many of the members, past and present, continues to be a source of pride to the organization. The members listed in various *Who's Who* and similar publications are extraordinary in a club of this size in a village of 28,000. In 2010, members listed their affiliations with fifty-two state, regional, and national organizations, including specific professional *Who's Whos*. Seven current members of the Club have been or are currently listed in the prestigious national Marquis *Who's Who in America*.

It is perhaps unfair to select only a few names for comment, for it is impossible to point out every member, past and present, who has achieved national distinction. Nevertheless, a few persons in widely diverse fields, need to be mentioned.

A prime benefactor of the Club was R. T. Miller, who joined in 1942. He sparked the Club's practice of giving scholarship aid to Rollins students, and he was a frequent large lender and donor to Club projects and the frequent "anonymous" donor in the early days. He was an educator and publisher.

Arthur M. Harris, who built the Little Harris Clubhouse as a surprise to the members in 1937, appears not to have been a college graduate, although he was presented with an honorary LL.D. from Dennison University in 1936. He is listed as having been a banker, with his office on Madison Avenue in New York City.

Another early member, Dr. Louis I. Dublin, was Chief Statistician and Vice President of the Metropolitan Life Insurance Company. Through his researches and activism he became the world's authority on public health and established many of the standards that affect everyone today.

Dr. Paul S. Olmstead joined the Club in 1965. He was the designer of a statistical quality control and sampling system, especially in the theory of runs, which eliminated the existing practice of one hundred percent inspection of manufactured goods.

Charles S. Duffy served as President in 1975-1976 and also served several terms as Vice President for Programs. During that time he and his wife, Faith, planned and organized the popular "Mystery Tours." He named the monthly newsletter *Club Time* and was its first editor. He was followed by Walter Zimmerman who was later joined as coeditor by Robert Wilkinson (President 1980-1981). When Zimmerman stepped down, Richard Sewell (President 1996-1998) joined as coeditor. In spite of some changes in styles over the years for the publication, it has remained more or less as Duffy started it.

The newsletter has, however, changed its schedule of publication. It had been published on an erratic schedule since its inception in 1975. In 2001, the issues went to a once-a-month publication. And Dan Schulz (President 2004-2006) added an "s" to the word "*Time*" in the title of the publication.

In recent years there have been other notable members. Tom Polgar, long with the CIA as a Station Chief in various foreign countries, has been a member since 1983, and is a frequent speaker to Club audiences. He also adds his knowledgeable insights to Current Events discussions.

But the question of the type of organization the University Club should be has always been a recurring theme. As previously noted, in the very early days of the Club, the question of admitting nondegreed men to membership was a controversial subject. Partisanship was strong on each side, with the decision finally to admit one nondegreed member for every ten degree-holders.

In 2010, some twelve percent of the members did not have a college degree. They were admitted on the basis of life experience under a quota of twenty percent of the number of new members that had been accepted in the previous twelve months.

There is often pressure to recruit younger members. Members of whatever age are always welcome. But what is usually meant by "younger members" is that 50- to 60-something persons should be asked to join.

The Club grows, changes, and resolves differences as its members dictate. Many believe that there is a sense that life's pageant is rich and fuller with human contact at the Club. And withal there is accommodation, learning, respect, comity, and a large measure of affection.

CHAPTER 13

The Indispensable Staff

The earliest reference to a staff person is a letter of reminiscence written by Member Clarence Day on the occasion of the twentieth anniversary of the founding of the Club. As previously noted, in the collection of papers written for that occasion, he wrote that he and Al Dorn had spent all morning of May 25, 1948 closing up the Little Harris Clubhouse for good. Mr. Dorn had been a part-time paid helper for some time at that Clubhouse, and he moved with the furnishings to the new building a block away.

As Member Paul Beik noted later, "At that time the University Club consisted of 443 members, and was proceeding confidently into its fourteenth year." It was evident that with the new large Clubhouse and extensive grounds, some further paid staff would be essential. The references to staff persons are imprecise, but it is apparent that the need for someone full-time in the office was becoming increasingly obvious.

And by the time the Club began its twenty-sixth year, Miriam Shaw was already reliably fulfilling the duties of office manager in support of member-generated activities. In addition, Mrs. Shaw was performing the duties of secretary, invoicing clerk, and general expediter of the Club's affairs. Mrs. Shaw retired in 1965 at the age of 81.

She was succeeded by Esther (Spence) Woods, who served until 1972. But some problems surfaced during her tenure. A special meeting of members was called in August of 1968 to consider the case of a custodial employee whose excessive drinking had caused Mrs. Cread Ellison (hired to replace Esther during her vacation) to resign after one week, necessitating the early return of Esther. After considering the custodian's long history of insobriety, it was decided to discharge him. But this was a rare and unfortunate instance. Most of the custodial employees had received commendatory mention in the minutes.

After 1972, the position in the office was filled by several temporary employees until Member Lucienne Lynas (now Lee) agreed to help out temporarily in 1978. As Member Paul Beik wrote, "She managed to escape into retirement in 1983."

Harry Lynas came to the Club as Custodian in 1973 and was in that position when the Club turned fifty. He became a member of the Club in 1974, but remained as general overseer of the functions of the Club until 1989, having various others under his direction to oversee both the interior and exterior of the building.

After an interval when several custodians worked for a short period, Richard Sevick came to the Club in 1990 as Facilities Manager. The complicated scheduling of functions in the Clubhouse is the responsibility of this position, as well as seeing that the Clubhouse is clean, in order, and presentable. He was assisted on a part-time basis by his son, James Sevick, who attended to the mowing of the grass and to other tasks outside and inside the Clubhouse at the direction of the Facilities Manager.

On May 1, 1996, LaVaughn (Sam) Parrish was hired as Custodian to assist the Facilities Manager. The duties of the new position consisted of lawn maintenance and miscellaneous indoor tasks.

Richard Sevick resigned as Facilities Manager in May 1999 to accept other employment. His successor, Brent Howard, was hired, and resigned a year-and-a-half later. Howard was replaced by David Hendricks in 2000 who stayed until 2005.

Manuel Sauri, a native of Peru, joined the Club staff as Facilities Manager on February 14, 2005.

A detailed study done in 2005 regarding the cost of the custodial position showed that if the position were abolished, $8,000 could be saved in that fiscal year and $18,000 in the following year (including the cost of a private contractor). The savings from this change would be the equivalent of gaining seventy-five new members. In the interest of economizing, it was decided that an outside contractor would be hired to maintain the Club grounds. Sam Parrish was terminated with severance pay in September 2005. He was missed by many Club members.

Jan Anderson came to the Club as Office Manager in 1984, succeeding Lucienne Lynas (Lee) as the Club was celebrating its fiftieth birthday. She streamlined the increasingly complicated office functions, endearing herself to everyone in the process. She occasionally had part-time help. After nearly fifteen years of service to the Club as Office Manager, she retired in 1998.

Holly Milton, her replacement, was hired as Office Administrator on March 11, 1998. Penny Benet-Denny, a part-time office employee, resigned shortly after that, and a second position for the office was authorized by the Board. On May 18, 1998, Rebecca Van Horn was employed as Assistant Office Administrator.

Through the years, office machines were added to lighten the load of routine tasks. Persuading the Board that such equipment was necessary was sometimes difficult. At one time the need for an electric typewriter to replace the old manual one was debated and the purchase delayed for a time. Even as late as the mid-1980s, the Board was vetoing the purchase of a copier for cost-effective reasons, but one was finally acquired. In 1987 the first computer was purchased, greatly facilitating record-keeping.

After the arrival of Holly Milton and Rebecca Van Horn in 1998, the Club gradually entered the computer age. A new computer was purchased, a second one was upgraded, and another was obtained for the President's office. This advanced equipment made a noticeable difference in the office workload, and the individual responsibilities for each employee were more clearly defined by the Human Resources Committee in 2007.

As Office Administrator, Holly Milton is the overall Administrator for the Club staff. In this capacity, she ensures that the staff meets the high standards of the Club. She oversees all phases of Club rentals, meets and greets prospective renters, and coordinates actions of Club officers and the Facilities Manager.

Her responsibilities to the Club President include preparation of correspondence, reporting on events or situations that require attention, and ensuring that the President and Human Resources Committee are informed of any issue regarding the staff.

In support of dinners, luncheons, and brunches, she maintains the answering machine message, keeps a list of attendees and tallies numbers, assists the seating committee, the greeters, and the cashiers; and makes money deposits.

For the Vice Presidents of Membership and other Committees, she prepares all correspondence on new members and on resignations, illness, deaths, memorials, deletions, and address changes. And she provides assistance and support to the membership committee.

Rebecca Van Horn continues to serve as the Assistant Office Administrator and the staff Financial Officer in 2010. She develops and maintains all financial records, including monthly database reports, payroll records, and transactions with banks. She has responsibility for the monthly *Club Times*, which includes a schedule of all Club events and activities, and she keeps *Yearbook* information current on the database. Her support for the Vice President of Development includes preparation of annual appeals, monthly reports on all contributions and lists for *Club Times* as required, and Development Committee correspondence. Year-end reports for membership, dues notifications, and lists of unpaid dues are also her responsibility.

The two office staff members work interchangeably; one covers for the other during absences. Despite frequent interruptions with telephone calls and visitors, the work goes on; deadlines are met and projects are completed. Nonetheless, visitors and members are greeted with a smile. Perhaps more important, these two employees are always gracious and ready to offer assistance to the new (and old) members.

The Facilities Manager's duties have become more time-consuming in recent years due to the increase in the number of Intellectual Activities Groups and rentals and the additional audio-visual equipment. Manuel Sauri is responsible for keeping the Clubhouse in good condition—always orderly and clean. He maintains an accurate schedule of the various functions and meetings, and performs set-up and take-down service for all Club and most rental events. He operates the stage lighting along with the audio and video systems at many events. He performs minor repairs on the plumbing system, electrical systems, and the structure, and obtains and evaluates bids and recommends action to the House and Grounds Vice President for contractor services.

He also maintains an inventory of equipment and building supplies, and purchases replacement supplies, works rental events, and is responsible for training and supervising the part-time employees who handle custodial and audio-visual duties during evening Club events. And he works closely with the landscaping people as well as the various service folk who are called from time to time for maintenance and repair tasks. It is a never-ending task that requires physical activity, organization, and managerial ability. Club members are very appreciative of his cooperation and service to the Club.

Between 1997 and 2001, two new benefits were approved for the Club Staff: (1) on January 1, 1997, a health insurance plan was selected for employees, with the Club paying one hundred percent of the insurance premium. Later, the Board approved the payment of fifty percent of the premium for dependents up to a cap of $250 a month. (2) On May 1, 2001, employees were authorized to open an Individual Retirement Account, to which the Club makes an annual contribution.

The Human Resources Committee was created at the May 9, 2000 meeting of the Executive Board. It consists of three members and the President (who serves *ex officio*). The House and Grounds Vice President is also an *ex officio* member when matters relating to the Facility Manager are under discussion. The Committee reports to the Club President.

The Human Resources Committee (proficiently chaired for many years by Member Herb Smetheram) is responsible for making specific recommendations regarding compensation, paid time-off policies, holiday schedules, and other personnel matters to the Board for each employee, and for the formal position descriptions, ensuring that they are kept current. Employees are informed that the Human Resources Committee is their point of contact for work-related issues and concerns.

As noted by Past President Donald Meckstroth (President 1995-1996), "much, but not enough, has been said of the University Club's staff." The Club is very fortunate to have these outstanding employees who are consistently loyal, cooperative, and dedicated to the best interests of the Club. They are truly "the indispensable staff."

The Indispensable Staff: Manuel Sauri, Holly Milton, Rebecca Van Horn

CHAPTER 14

Prized Possessions

The Club has acquired some valued possessions, and tradition and sentiment are centered around them.

After the move to the present Clubhouse, the lectern (or as it was called in the early years, the reading desk) was purchased by Member Hamilton Gibson in 1948, who thought that the platform/stage in the auditorium of the new Clubhouse should have such a piece. The design was approved (a complicated one with a ratchet arrangement for adjusting both the height and the slant of the shelf) by the Board. The lectern is still used at all meetings in the Auditorium.

The piece so pleased Mr. Gibson that he expressed a desire for some handsome chairs to flank it on the platform. A pair of antique Spanish armchairs was found, for which he was happy to pay. He financially supported their refinishing, repairing, and reupholstering. The chairs fell into disrepair and disuse, but in 1994 another member had them retrieved from the basement of the Clubhouse and paid for their repair, refinishing, and reupholstering. Unfortunately, the chairs later became infested with termites and were destroyed. Replacements were acquired, but lacked the charming history (see Chapter 3).

The photographic portrait of the first president, Dr. George M. Whicher, was presented to the Club by his wife following his death in 1939. The portrait was first displayed in the Little Harris Clubhouse, then was moved to the new Clubhouse. Many years ago it vanished into the projection booth above the auditorium. It was water-stained and the flimsy  frame had also suffered. In 1994 it was retrieved by Facilities Manager Richard Sevick, who brought it to the attention of a member. The portrait was cleaned by an artist-member and retouched by another member, who also paid for its proper framing—complete with an identifying brass plaque. It now hangs in the Boardroom.

The Club has two gavels. The first was presented to the Club in 1939 by Member H. K. Hawley. A story surrounds the other gavel, which has become the official one.

The former home of President of the United States William McKinley in Canton, Ohio fell into such disrepair that it had to be razed. A quantity of lumber sections were salvaged from the front porch. At the suggestion of William Mills, later a member of the Club, to Dallas L. Hostetler (also later a member but at that time manager of the Canton Chamber of Commerce), a limited number of gavels were made from this wood by manual-training students in one of the high schools.

One such gavel was used to open the Republican National Convention in Cleveland in June of 1936. Another is in the Smithsonian Institution. Still another was given to Mr. Mills and Mr. Hostetler also received one.

The following remarks are in a memo dated January 11, 1969 from Edgerton B. Williams (President 1968-1969):

Henceforth it shall be known as the McKinley-Hostetler Gavel and it is ordered that same shall be used to officially open and close business meetings of the Club and also meetings of the Executive Committee thereof.

A tradition developed that the gavel is publicly transferred from the President to the President Elect at the Annual General Meeting, and again at the last dinner of the fiscal year.

A self-leveling dictionary stand was designed and constructed by Edger S. Nethercut, who presented it to the Club November 3, 1951. It was used for many years in the Library, but since has been retired and replaced by a smaller stand.

The Steinway grand piano was acquired in April of 1988 from the estate of Arthur Normandin, a member from 1964 until his death. The Club had the instrument put into top playing condition, and had installed on the side a brass plaque reading:

**Dedicated to the memory of
G. Arthur Normandin,
Member 1964-1988**

A letter from Steinway and Sons in New York dated November 6, 1991 states that this 6-foot 10-inch Model B Grand in ebonized finish was manufactured in New York in 1908. The more-than-102-year-old instrument (in 2010) was pronounced "not in bad shape" by a piano tuner that year.

The piano replaced a former grand piano, which was in less-than-concert condition. On one occasion Pianist Gary Wolfe, faculty member at the University of Central Florida, was playing a recital in the auditorium, and several ivories flew off the keys, to the embarrassment of the members.

In 2010, Club Member Joseph Rubel generously presented the Club with a gift of a new Steinway-designed upright piano. It was greatly appreciated.

A set of prints from watercolors by Windon S. Newton was presented to the Club in 1987 and hung in the Boardroom.

This collection, depicting Rollins College campus scenes, was a gift from Club Member Thaddeus Seymour, former President of Rollins College, and his wife Polly.

On the walls of the Library, several recognition plaques honor members for their service to the Club. The wall clock on the west side of the Library was a gift to the Club from Vee Florea in memory of her husband, President Emeritus Harold Florea (1983-1984). It strikes every hour and chimes each quarter of an hour, but both have been disconnected because the noise was disturbing to many members during programs in the Library. This beautiful, useful gift was received in 1998.

The table now in the Boardroom was the gift of the Barnett Bank in 1987. It was uncomfortably large for the room at the time that it was acquired, but it fit splendidly into the new and enlarged Boardroom that was a part of the 1992-1994 renovation and expansion.

Also in the Boardroom there are decorative scrolls containing the names and years of service of the Past Presidents. These beautiful scrolls are the work of Virgil Hartsock (President 1981-1982).

Another treasure is the Club songbook. The book, copyrighted in 1945, was titled *Songs of the University Club* and was printed by the College Press at 415 Fairbanks Avenue. The work contains nine original songs, with music by Henry Dyke Sleeper, retired professor of music at Smith College and editor of the first Harvard song book in 1886. The words were written by Royal Wilbur France, attorney and member of the New York bar, who came to Rollins as Professor of Economics in 1929. One of his original works was the Club song, "O Club of Universities." This number, although dated, was brought out of retirement and performed several times by the Men's Chorus under the direction of George Grace and at Club dinners in 2008-2009.

As mentioned in earlier pages, singing was a large part of the dinner programs during the first twenty or so years of the Club's existence and at most meetings the diners were serenaded by the "Men of Song" or the "Boy's Choir." The songbook was therefore an important, valued possession. As far as is known, only one copy still exists.

Another musical treasure is the "University Fanfare," composed specifically for the University Club by world-class musician and composer Sergei Kossenko, a friend of Joe Rizzo (President 2006-2007), and a frequent performer at and suporter of the Club.

The work was written for Brass Quintet and had its world premiere at the dinner on April 9, 2010, as a part of the 75th Anniversary celebration. It was performed by the Orlando Brass Quintet. A copy of the work is in the Club Library.

A member's gift of an American flag and a 40-foot flagpole was accepted by the Board in February 1954. It anchors the Park and Webster corner of the Club grounds.

The Club has had many artists among its members, and works by a few are on display, notably watercolors by Members Dot Cline, Daphne Frutchey, George Stewart, Nita Marie Rizzo, and others, which grace the premises.

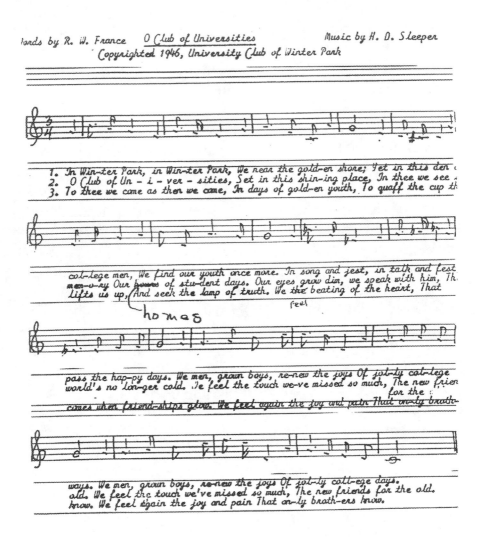

The Club song, "O Club of Universities" with words by
Roy Wilbur France and music by Henry Dyke Sleeper (1945)

"University Fanfare for Brass Quintet"
Composed for the University Club of Winter Park
on the occasion of its 75th Anniversary, by Sergei Kossenko
World Premiere on April 8, 2010

A review of the posses-sions around which many of the Club's traditions center has some plaintive aspects. There have been two gongs given to the Club, and both have been used to call to order and dismiss meetings. The first is the Chinese gong, the second is Japanese. The Chinese gong is a flanged disc of etched brass about nine inches in diameter suspended by thongs from a footed bronze frame. This gong is struck with a padded mallet, which produces a somewhat tinny sound having little re-verberation.

With the arrival of the Japanese gong in 1954, the small Chinese gong was ig-nominiously retired. And then someone thought of the Woman's Club. That organizaion had no gong. Should not their meetings be called to order by means of the sound of a gong?

The Chinese Gong

So the Chinese gong was given to the Woman's Club with the proviso that it should be returned when and if ever it was not used. Officers of organizations change. And the Woman's Club, after a few years, quietly retired the gong to a storage closet, its history by then forgotten. It was even included in their annual Flea Market. There were no customers for it.

Then a University Club member, visiting the Woman's Club one day, chanced to look in the closet and remarked that the gong really belonged to the University Club and should be returned as long as it was not being used. So the gong was polished and returned with thanks in 1976. Since then it has sat on a shelf in the Library at the University Club. It was pol-ished and shown at the dinner on August 27, 1993 in the charge of the Club History Committee. It was again polished and shining and on display at the Gala Diamond Jubilee dinner on March 27, 1994. Today, the gong calls the members at the predinner reception in the Library to dinner in the Auditorium.

The Japanese gong was once used to open and close all meetings in the Auditorium. It was originally lent to the Club

by Dr. Waite Allison Cotton, a retired dentist. From the shape of the gong, it is understandable that it was sometimes referred to, a bit irreverently, as the "Cotton Bowl." Dr. Cotton spent some time in the Orient and acquired the gong in Japan. When struck on the inside of the rim with the padded mallet, it produces a mellow resonating tone that echoes for many seconds.

It was the understanding of both Dr. Cotton and the Club that the loan of the gong would become permanent upon his death. But, someone, not knowing how the gong should be struck, hit it mightily on the side and produced a dent. This so enraged Dr. Cotton that he took the gong home, and there it stayed until his death in 1970 at the age of 95. He had willed the gong to a friend. The friend, having little use for such an accessory, gave it back to the Club. The base is gone, but the gong is on display at the Club.

The Japanese Gong

Another prized possession is the plaque near the Webster Avenue entrance, designating the building as a Winter Park landmark. President George Wannall (2002-2003) requested of Diane Sandquist (President 2001-2002) that she work with the city to seek

this honor. This was accomplished on May 27, 2003 with the City Council designating the building as an "historic landmark on the Winter Park Register of Historic Places."

The most prized possession of the Club is the mural at the back of the stage on the front wall of the Auditorium. Titled "New York Bay," it is from an original painting by the French artist Jean-Julien Deltil in the 1820s, according to Fred Rosenthal (President 2003-2004), who did extensive research on the painting. Based on Deltil's engravings, this is one of four panels that were combined to present "Vue d'Amerique du Nord" and were installed in the White House in the 1960s, during the Kennedy administration.

The block print was made by Zuber et Cie and bought in France in 1963 by Club Member Robert Jacobson. He was an architect and interior designer who worked with Frank Lloyd Wright for years in the Chicago-Milwaukee area. It was his intention to install the mural in a home he intended to build for himself, but that was not accomplished. He moved to Florida and became a member of the University Club and was very active, but had a stroke and was moved to the Nursing Center of the Winter Park Towers. A month before he died on December 5, 1992 he asked John Bond (also a member of the Club), to retrieve a round container from his closet, which held the eight rolls of block print wallpaper. He wanted the Club to have it.

The print was first known as "The Promenade." Officially it had been known as "New York Bay" or "General View of New York." Other sources depict it as "Manhattan," with a skyline punctuated by church spires as seen from across the Hudson on the fashionable promenade on Weekhawken Heights, New Jersey. Well-dressed people are depicted, both white and black, strolling, on horseback, and in a carriage. It is a remarkable possession.

The Club has acquired some prized possessions during its 75 years, but it continues the tradition of the premise that the organization's most prized possessions are its members.

The Mural

CHAPTER 15

Celebrations and History Books

The first mention of a celebration marking years of activity in the Clubhouse was a review of the programs held to observe twenty years of its existence. Perhaps those early years had been too full of activity; perhaps concerns about the war years (those of both World War II and the Korean Conflict) had crowded out thoughts of anniversary celebrations. Perhaps it required a full twenty years to provoke reminiscences.

The first recorded observance of a significant anniversary of the Club occurred in 1954, with celebrations on March 23 (a Powwow), on March 26 (also a Powwow), and on March 27 with a business meeting in the evening.

All three of these occasions consisted of personal accounts of events during the past years, most of them papers written and delivered by former Presidents. The papers have been preserved in their original form in a loose-leaf binder with the title "Lest We Forget." The information in these papers was invaluable in putting together the first two histories of the Club, as well as this update.

There is no suggestion that luncheons or dinners or other social events were included in the early observances. There were, however, two poems written by members for the celebration. One was titled "The Spirit of the Occasion," and the other "Rendezvous." The original pages of "Lest We Forget" are in fragile condition. They are in the Club Library.

By the time of the twenty-fifth anniversary, at least one person was feeling the necessity for a more formal written record. William E. Stark (President 1956-1957), who had been a founding member and who had served for some years as Recording Secretary, took it upon himself to write a history of the first twenty-five years. This is a charming and personal account of the beginnings of the Club as seen through his eyes.

This book was titled *The First Twenty-Five Years of the University Club of Winter Park* and was issued in hard cover in 1959 and was available for sale at $1.00. The initial cost of publication was underwritten by a generous Anonymous Donor, his original intent being that whatever proceeds resulted from sales would go to the Club treasury. However, it was the feeling of the members that such money should be used to repay, at least in part, the gift. The final details are not clear. But the book was produced, many copies were sold to members, and the Club Library was the happy recipient of a number of copies. The copies in the library are available for perusal by today's members.

As the date of the fiftieth anniversary approached, there were suggestions that some observance should be made. One of the members was designated to update the Stark history, perhaps amplifying it from the available records and reviewing the succeeding fifteen years. This was not accomplished.

The celebration of the Golden Anniversary of the Club, however, was considerably more elaborate than the previous observances had been. It was, after all, a milestone.

This time, again, there were hopes for a new history of the Club. The President, Hal Florea (1983-1984), made notes to begin such a work; many pages of notes from the records were also made by member Paul Beik. No pages of copy ever resulted, but the notes have been useful in compiling subsequent history books of the Club.

A handsome logo was designed in 1983 by artist Members Charles Turzak and Dorothy Hales with a motto written by Hal Florea (President 1983-1984). This logo is still in use on stationery and other printed materials, the Club blazer patch, polo shirts, and for all Club promotions and publications. And it graces the cover of this book.

Prior to any celebrations, the groundwork for them had been laid the previous year. In May of 1983 a Fiftieth Anniversary Committee was formed, and the following September there is in the record the first mention of a "Golden Flame" (for Club improvement). In October a letter was sent to the membership soliciting funds for the Golden Flame. The money raised from the fund drive ($18,000) was intended to be used to "face-lift" the aging building. In May 1984, $6,500 of that money was used to paint the inside and outside of the building. The rest went for other Club improvements (see Chapter 4).

And there were gala events. The Mayor of Winter Park at that time, Hope Strong, issued a proclamation declaring the week of March 19-24, 1984, to be "The University Club of Winter Park Week," and all citizens were encouraged to share in the event. Among other things, the Club was recognized in the proclamation for "its long dedication to community services, as well as intellection [sic]."

On March 18 of the same year the Club held an Open House. Club President Hal Florea made opening remarks, and the Mayor read the proclamation. The founders were recognized and the participation of those founders who were also members of Rollins College faculty and staff was acknowledged by Rollins President Thaddeus Seymour, a member of the Club. Recognition of the Chamber of Commerce participation was similarly acknowledged by Chamber President Michael Marlowe. The Past Presidents of the Club were recognized and Virgil Hartsock, the Immediate Past President, acknowledged the recognition.

The final celebration of the Golden Anniversary was the gala luncheon for Club members and their guests at the Maison & Jardin Restaurant in Altamonte Springs on March 24, 1984. All in all, the Golden Anniversary was a memorable one.

As the sixtieth anniversary of the founding approached, the desire to have a newer and more comprehensive written history arose again. In the fall of 1992, President Erwin Britton appointed a committee charged with the task of writing a new history covering the first sixty years. That committee, known as the Ad Hoc Club History Committee, met at regular (and sometimes irregular) times, dividing the work of reading and digesting original source material, having complete copies of one anothers' work, agreeing on a suggested outline, and intending to arrive at a completed manuscript in timely fashion for publication on the founding date of March 4 or thereabouts. This date was later altered in order to be able to include in the book the account of the Diamond Jubilee (60th) festivities.

The research proved more complicated than had been anticipated, partly because of the condition of the records, partly because of competing commitments of the committee members, and partly because some of the material proved so interesting that unexpected amounts of time were spent in pursuing amusing, but somewhat extraneous, details. (It is noted that a similar pattern emerged with preparation of this volume in 2009-2010.)

The first Club meeting devoted to the history up to 1994 took place on August 27, 1993 at a dinner meeting chaired by Member Alice Britton and attended by many Club members. The program consisted of a talk about some of the amusing anecdotes from the Club's past and a display of some of the Club artifacts. These included the Japanese (Cotton) gong that had been used for many years and also the smaller gong that preceded it (the Chinese gong), the two Club gavels, the photograph of the first President (then in deplorable condition), the reading desk (the podium), the antique Spanish chairs (which had been a part of the original furnishings of the new Clubhouse), and other items — all with details of their histories.

Work on the history book continued, with frequent meetings of the committee. Research materials were shared among all members.

The Board decided early in the winter of 1994 that finishing the book should be delayed until after the Diamond Jubilee celebration, which was planned to be a dinner at the Club on the evening of March 25 with an open house and art show at the Clubhouse on the afternoon of March 27.

The dinner was the responsibility of the Club History Committee, but the art show and reception were a joint undertaking of the Club History, Program, and Interior Arts Committees. The dinner was a black-tie affair. Unfortunately, not all those who wished to attend could be accommodated, because there simply was not room.

A special menu was arranged with the Club caterer, Leona Paul of Classic Creations. (Classic Creations has been the Club caterer since 1991.) Place cards were provided for every person attending. The flowers and vases were donated by a member, and the flower arrangements were given to someone at each of the tables.

The photographic portrait of the first President, George Whicher, which had been discovered in a storeroom in poor condition was cleaned, retouched, properly framed, and unveiled by Radmilla Graham, wife of then President Chet Graham (1993-1994). The cost of the restoration and framing was paid by a member of the Club, and the portrait was presented to the Club as an important artifact.

Chair Alice Britton introduced all the Past Presidents that were present. Each of them gave short remarks having to do with some event in his administration. The Past Presidents, speaking in the order of their seniority were Ross Pollock, Gil Buhrmann, Robert Wilkinson, Hal Florea, Walter Tolson, John Bond, David Stonecliffe, John Heiland, J. B. Lea, and "Brit" Britton. The health of Past Presidents August Johansen (1972-1973) and Frank Linn (1974-1975) was too frail for them to attend. And two Past Presidents, Virgil Hartsock (1981-1982) and Joseph Terranova (1990-1991) were out of the country.

The Club Poem, written long ago, was read by member John Budlong, who sang the final stanza—to the tune of "America the Beautiful." Alas, copies of the poem have been lost to antiquity.

Because there had been no budget for the program or decorations, the Committee was pleased to have received enough donations for the Club to pay for these aspects of the celebration as well as new carafes for the dinner tables and enough tumblers to provide glasses for every diner to have one for water *and* one for iced tea.

Alice Britton and President Graham, 1984

President Chet Graham presented to Alice Britton at the end of the program a plaque expressing gratitude for her work. This was a complete surprise, and was accepted in the name of the Club History Committee.

The dinner was a true gala — an event that brought happiness and joy to the participants, and pride to the Club. And the celebration continued.

The next day, March 26, was a busy one. The art show of members' works, which had been hung in the Gallery since early in March, was taken down and in its place different works by Club members, living and deceased, were mounted. There were paintings in various media.

Also on display in the Gallery and in the auditorium were embroideries, elaborate decorated eggs (after the manner of Cellini), wood sculptures, a sculpted self-portrait, books written by members, other sculptures, paintings, and books not in the Library.

On Sunday afternoon, March 27, the members and guests attended the Open House. All the food had been prepared and donated by members of the History and Program Committees. This was another happy party, attended by a great many — and obviously enjoyed, because there was no food left from the great quantity that had been provided.

Because the unabridged dictionary designates both sixtieth and seventy-fifth anniversaries as Diamond events, the Club looked forward to Diamond II in fifteen years.

And as the 75th Anniversary approached in 2009, it was decided that a year — and longer — recognition of the Club's history should be celebrated. Under the leadership of Frank Paul Barber (President 2008-2009) the Club honored itself with four events surrounding the beginnings of the Club. In anticipation of the celebrations, wine glasses embossed with the Club name were donated by an anonymous contributor in 2007, and champagne glasses were donated in 2008.

So in 2009, concerts, dances, and a brunch were scheduled in a jam-packed weekend. On April 3 Miss Jacqueline Jones, renowned jazz singer, brought down the full house with a concert, followed by the Orlando Opera Company the next evening for another black-tie sellout crowd. The weekend was capped with a Sunday brunch and dancing to the Julie Lyon Quartet on April 5.

The celebration continued later in the month with a concert by the Men's Chorus, directed by George Grace and chaired by Member Malcolm Frazier, the afternoon of April 17. They managed to complete "75 Songs in 75 Minutes for 75 Years," beginning with the pop songs of the day from 1934.

A few months later, Max Reed (President 2009-2010) appointed a 75th Anniversary Committee, coordinated by Diane Sandquist (President 2001-2002) as the Club sought to continue its celebration in partnership with Rollins College, which was celebrating its 125th anniversary, and the Bach Festival, celebrating its 50th anniversary.

That Committee scheduled another gala weekend celebration in January of 2010, which featured Rollins College musicians in a recital conducted by John Sinclair, the Director of the Bach Festival and good friend of the Club. Distinguished guests at that Friday luncheon on January 15 were Rollins faculty members and the Bach Festival Board; all were recognized from the podium.

At a festive black-tie dinner the next evening Member Thad Seymour, Past President of Rollins and Club Member, delivered a reminiscence about the close relationship between Rollins College and the Club. Honoring our youth, dinner music was provided by No Smoking — a high school jazz group. Both events played to sold-out audiences.

At the Saturday dinner, the Club recognized the organizations that were instrumental in creating the Club and the Financial Luncheons. The Club's Past Presidents that were in attendance were also honored.

The 75th Anniversary Committee subsequently appointed a subcommittee to work on an update of the Club's History, chaired by stalwart Member Mary Keck. That committee's work has resulted in this book.

The members of the Club look forward to future celebrations of its founding and history and to another written history of the Club. It has been a remarkable journey of a unique institution.

Thad Seymour, 2010

Pride in the Past—Faith in the Future

Retrospective and Prospective

By Bob Reed

Born in the Great Depression and living in the Great Recession, the University Club endures. It holds steadfast to its purpose and traditions in 2010.

It has experienced the best and worst of times in the life of the country. But the merry band of a winter colony — grayhaired men who founded the organization — would hopefully recognize their offspring.

They were serious intellectuals with a wry sense of self-depreciating humor, in spite of their great career accomplishments. Their dedication to what became known as continuing education was remarkable. Those who had convened in barbershops found a new venue.

Their devotion to intellectual stimulation in their declining years and their passion for the personal camaraderie of friendship and human intercourse were their motivations. It was a simpler time in the midst of an economic depression.

Their successors survived World War II, the Korean Conflict, and the Vietnam and Gulf wars. And they have seen major changes in the culture of the country and its citizens in the 75 years of Club existence. The accumulated sorrows of all those wars created a solidarity among people and a need for sharing and companionship.

Many of today's members also grew up in periods of want and unpaved roads, and of the box without a screen called the radio. They listened to "Jack Armstrong," wore bobby sox, sang songs from "Your Hit Parade," and later adapted to the war protestors of the '60s, long hair on men, the feminist movement, and sexual freedom.

It was an era where connectivity did not require a USB cable. Those members saw the appearance of the Pill, and grass that didn't grow on the lawn. And they accommodated environmental changes in a world they remembered in which sex was dirty and the air was clean, not the other way around.

They adjusted to television, moon walks, and political shenanigans and scandals in the '70s and '80s. But by the '90s, it became easier for the members to stay home and watch television for four hours and thirty-five minutes a day (which is the national average) than to get up out of the chair and make it to the Club. And many of the aging membership found it difficult to drive, particularly at night.

By 2010 the members of the Club and the citizens of the nation and the world were challenged to further adapt to the digital revolution in the forms of new media. From the earlier decades of just film and radio, we entered a new era of seemingly unlimited choices. It's now a time of technological and cultural change. The pace is fast. Multitasking is the rage.

The impact of modern technology in the use of computers and hand-held devices is startling. Tweeting and Facebook and the use of smart phones occupy many hours of the day. Some statistics show a threefold increase in the consumption of "media" between 1996 and 2008.

There is an electronic flood, an array of bewildering devices. And the public and many members of the Club struggle with the effects of this deluge of information.

This electronic environment is hardly passive. It is responsive and informative, not unlike spoken discourse in the real world. You can Google anything. Information is at our fingertips and it causes some trepidation.

It's a familiar human problem, dating back to at least the Greeks. Socrates, the greatest of all oral communicators, railed over the growing phenomenon of written language, based on the alphabet. He believed that scrolls wouldn't allow ideas to flow freely, changing as they do in conversations. This philosophy also prevailed in ancient Ireland.

New forms of media have always caused moral and cultural panics—the printing press, newspapers, paperback books, radio, and television were often denounced as threats to a person's brainpower and moral fiber.

When comic books were accused of turning kids into delinquents in the 1950s, however, crime was falling to record lows. The denunciations of video games in the 1990s also coincided with a crime decline. And the decades of television, transistor radios, and rock videos was a time in which I.Q. scores rose. The deleterious effects of consuming today's electronic media are far more limited than any panic implies.

But their effect on the world, its citizens, and on the Club is worrisome. Knowledge is increasing exponentially. The Internet and other information devices are helping us manage, search, and retrieve intellectual output at different scales—from Twitter to on-line encyclopedias. We can find everything about anything.

In 2007 the Club accepted the donation of two computers to assist in that process. And it developed the training by and for members, to use them.

But the habits of discussion and the immediate reaction to statements, criticism, rigorous debate, and sallies are often missing. These are the province of the Intellectual Activities— the soul of the Club. Many members want to feel of and in the moment and maintain that these small group interchanges are the major benefits of Club membership. They allow us to be truly human in activities that fulfill, give meaning to our lives, and enable us to more easily embrace those around us. It is indeed as the Club motto states: "Fellowship in Knowledge and Understanding."

Still, the decline in membership in the past few years is partially due to the availability and increase in the use of electronic media. And those changes have influenced the Club's leadership and membership as it faces further challenges.

Resulting cultural changes have also contributed to the decline in membership in the organization in the 21st century (see Chapter 12.) This is not a unique circumstance.

Membership in most civic organizations, including Rotary and Kiwanis, the Masons and many other groups—along with churches—has been in decline since the 1980s. Traditional country clubs have been struggling to maintain and recruit new members.

The societal changes are partially due to the new media. In 2008 people consumed three times as much information each day as they did in 1960. Why go out when you can watch the tube, order in, and exchange e-mail messages?

Supreme Court Justice Antonin Scalia noted in 2010 that "cell phone and text message communications are so pervasive that some persons may consider them to be essential means or necessary instruments for self-expression, even self-identification."

Some sociologists suggest other contributing factors to this new era of communication. They note the growing isolation among people—the fast pace of life where there are few speed limits, which creates a need for solitary leisure. And there is a raucous debate among scientists over whether this new technology's influence on behavior and the brain is good or bad.

For social intercourse has been invaded and sometimes occupied by the new media. Technology has often replaced the human interaction of people. And the Internet offers anonymity. As the saying goes, "No one knows you're a dog."

That privacy is appealing to many, but it diminishes social intercourse and collegiality. Technology often fills an emotional void, assuaging an inner blankness.

But even solitary activities have waned. Old pursuits like reading are in decline. Newspapers are struggling.

Relationships have come to play a diminished role in some lives. Many no longer seek the warmth of human contact.

The decline in membership in the Club in recent years is also due to a struggling economy, which has affected membership recruitment and retention. The modest dues are a burden to some retirees, near-retirees, and others.

But the Club continues to meet the challenges of this new world. It continues to try new recruitment methods, remembering that Noah had never before built an Ark but a group of professionals built the *Titanic*.

The Club is dedicated to intellectual exchange. And the leadership recognizes that the organization can never go back to before. So as the members and interests change, the Club has changed to meet them. It has been—and is—an evolving process, in an increasingly pluralistic world.

Its leaders constantly face a balancing act. Like the riders seated backwards on a train, looking out at what's already passed, they shift to a forward-facing seat to see what's currently passing and what is to come. In the middle of tomorrow, the Club strives to emerge from a distant yesterday.

The organization's purpose, however, remains to provide its members with a venue in which they can enjoy living the life they have earned. For many, the song they hear within themselves is alive and well, providing a gentle push for outreach. The Club continues to be a place where a member can be connected to others in a personal way—a place where hands touch hands and hearts smile and are warmly moved. And it remains—and will remain—a unique organization.

The attempt in these final words has been to provide a perspective on the Club, offering a context of where it has been, where it is, and where it is going. The Club's tense is in the future, for it has pride in the past and faith in that future.

APPENDICES

APPENDIX A

The 1937 Charter and 1941 Bylaws

The first printed membership list of the University Club was a booklet published in 1938 listing all the names and addresses, both temporary and permanent. The full text of the original charter and bylaws was also included and is reprinted here.

THE UNIVERSITY CLUB
OF WINTER PARK

The University Club of Winter Park was organized pursuant to a call by the College Committee of the Winter Park Chamber of Commerce. Under the leadership of Kenyon L. Butterfield the first meeting was held March 24, 1934.

The first program meeting was April 4. Under the constitution, adopted January 19, 1935, Dr. George M. Whicher was elected first President and James W. Newton Secretary-Treasurer, in which capacity he served three years until March, 1937.

In its present membership, one hundred colleges and universities are represented. Eight of these are in Europe. Educators constitute an impressive plurality with forty-five men registering under that classification. Businessmen, clergymen, lawyers, physicians and engineers are next in order. Of these, nineteen belong to Phi Beta Kappa; twenty-five have the degree of PhD, and fifty-nine are mentioned in Who's Who in America.

As a cross-section of academic America, the Club fills a unique place in the life of Winter Park. The assurance of its permanence and larger usefulness is increased by its recent incorporation and the erection of a new and attractive club house, in 1948.

ARTICLES OF INCORPORATION
(CONSTITUTION)

We, the undersigned incorporators do hereby associate ourselves together for the purpose of forming a corporation not for profit under the laws of the State of Florida and do hereby adopt the following articles of incorporation as the Charter for such association.

I

The name of this corporation shall be THE UNIVERSITY CLUB of WINTER PARK, and it shall be located in the City of Winter Park, Orange County, Florida.

II

The general nature of the object of the corporation shall be:

(a) To promote education and the attendance of proper persons at institutions of higher learning; to cultivate the artistic, scientific, and literary tastes and aspirations of the membership; to facilitate the social and intellectual intercourse of college men; and to aid and assist financially worthy students while seeking education.

III

Section 1. The membership of the Club shall consist of active members and such others as shall be prescribed by the by-laws of the Club.

Section 2. The active memberships shall be issued only to those persons who have regularly made application for membership in and have been accepted by the Club according to its by-laws.

Section 3. Admission to the Club shall be by vote of its members according to such rules and regulations relating thereto as may be fixed by the by-laws of the Club.

IV

The term for which this corporation shall exist shall be perpetual unless and until dissolved as it is now or may be hereafter provided by law.

V

The names and residences of the subscribers to these articles of incorporation are:

> George M. Whicher — Amherst, Mass.
> James W. Newton — Newton Center, Mass.
> Eugene R. Shippen — Winter Park, Fla.
> George W. Woodbury — Winter Park, Fla.
> Theodore E. Emery — Gardiner, Maine
> Edward M. Davis — Winter Park, Fla.
> Raymond W. Greene — Winter Park, Fla.

VI

Section 1. The affairs of this Club shall be managed by the duly elected officers of the Club in accordance with its by-laws.

Section 2. The officers of the Club shall be elected by the members from their membership at the regular annual meeting of the Club held on the day prescribed by the by-laws.

VII

The officers who are to manage the affairs of the Club until the first election held under this Charter shall be:

President   Edward M. Davis
Vice-President   George W. Woodbury
Secretary   Raymond W. Greene
Treasurer   Theodore E. Emery

VIII

The by-laws of this Club shall be made, altered, amended or rescinded by the members of the Club at any regular meeting by a vote of two-thirds of the members present at the regular meeting. When said by-laws are to be amended, altered or rescinded at any regular meeting, two weeks notice shall be given to all members of the proposed action to be taken.

IX

The highest amount of indebtedness or liability to which this corporation may at any time subject itself shall be the sum of $10,000.

X

The amount in value of the real estate which the corporation may hold, subject always to the approval of the Circuit Court Judge, shall be the sum of $10,000.

The foregoing articles in incorporation we subscribe this 12th day of April, A.D. 1937.

James W. Newton   George M. Whicher
George W. Woodbury   Eugene R. Shippen
Edward M. Davis   Theodore E. Emery
            Raymond W. Greene

THEREFORE ORDERED, ADJUDGED and DECREED that the foregoing charter be and the same is hereby approved, and "The University Club of Winter Park" be and it is from the date of the signing of this order, authorized to conduct its affairs as a fully organized corporation not for profit, with all the powers accorded to such corporation under the laws of the State of Florida.

DONE AND ORDERED in Chambers in Orlando, Orange County, Florida, this 13th day of April, A.D. 1937.

FRANK A. SMITH,
Judge.

BY-LAWS OF 1941

I. MEMBERSHIP

Section A. ADMISSION: Men who are permanent or temporary residents of Winter Park or vicinity and who hold a degree from a college or university or are graduates of the United States Military or the United States Naval Academy are eligible for membership and may be admitted to the Club by a three-fourths vote of the members present at any regular meetings; but a permanent or temporary resident of Winter Park or vicinity who does not hold a degree may be admitted to the Club upon a unanimous recommendation of the Membership Committee and by a three-fourths vote of the members present at any regular meeting. Members without degrees shall constitute not more than 10% of the total membership of the Club.

Section B. APPLICATIONS: All applications for membership shall be made in writing and signed by the member proposer. The full name, college, class, degree, profession, business, permanent and temporary address shall be given and delivered to the Committee on Membership for consideration. The name of a candidate not recommended by the Committee shall not be disclosed.

II. OFFICERS AND COMMITTEES

Section A. OFFICERS: The officers of the Club shall be a President, a Vice-President, a Secretary, a Treasurer and such other officers as the Club may determine to install. They shall perform the duties ordinarily associated with such offices in similar organizations. They shall be elected at the annual meeting for a term of one year, or until their successors shall have been elected and qualified.

Section B. STANDING COMMITTEES: There shall be four standing committees of not less than three or more than five members. Such committees shall be House, Membership, Memorials and Program. They shall be appointed by the President within two weeks after his election for a term of one year, or until their successors shall have been appointed and qualified. Other committees may be appointed from time to time by the President.

Section C. EXECUTIVE COMMITTEE: There shall be an Executive Committee consisting of the officers of the Club and the chairmen of the Standing Committees, which shall manage the affairs of the Club. The Executive Committee shall report to the Club at the first meeting of every month in which meetings are held.

The Executive Committee shall present for approval by the Club at the annual meeting a budget of the estimated receipts and expenditures for the ensuing year.

The Committee shall incur no financial obligations outside of the annual budget without first securing the approval of the Club.

Section D. NOMINATING COMMITTEE: A Nominating Committee of three members, not members of the Executive Committee shall be appointed by the President at the meeting preceding the annual meeting which shall bring in nominations for the officers for election at the annual meeting.

III. EXPENDITURES

EXPENDITURES: All expenditures shall be approved by the President or the Chairman of the appropriate committee and the accounts of the Treasurer shall be audited annually by an appointee of the President.

IV. MEETINGS

Section A. ANNUAL MEETING: The annual meeting shall be the first regular meeting in March.

Section B. REGULAR MEETINGS: Regular meetings of the Club shall be held on alternate Saturday evenings beginning with the first Saturday in December and ending with the first or second Saturday in April.

Section C. SPECIAL MEETINGS: Special meetings may be called by the President, by the Executive Committee, by a vote of the Club, or upon petition of at least 15 members.

Section D. QUORUM: For the transaction of business twenty-five members shall constitute a quorum.

Section E. NOTICES OF MEETINGS: Notification of all meetings shall be mailed to the members at least five days in advance of meetings.

V. DUES

Section A. ANNUAL DUES: The annual dues shall be $5.00 payable on or before January first of each fiscal year. Dues of members elected between January first and the annual meeting are payable within thirty days after election.

In the case of any member of the Club who after one season's residence in Winter Park or vicinity, is absent from the State of Florida throughout one or more entire seasons, his dues shall be $2.00 per year during the year or years of such absence; but upon his return for any part of any season to any place within the State of Florida, the regular rate of $5.00 shall again apply.

Section B. TERMINATION OF MEMBERSHIP: Membership shall cease if dues are not paid when due, but a membership that has ceased may be recovered by payment of unpaid and current dues.

The Treasurer shall send to all members whose dues are unpaid, at least thirty days prior to January 1, a notice which shall quote sections A and B of Article V of the By-Laws.

Section C. FISCAL YEAR: The fiscal year shall run from the annual meeting in March of each year until the next annual meeting.

(NOTE) AMENDMENTS: The By-Laws may be amended as provided for in Article VIII of the Charter.

APPENDIX B

Deed Restrictions

As a reflection of the time in which the University Clubhouse was built (1948), a review of the deed restrictions is instructive.

The lots purchased for the building at Webster and Park Avenues were a part of a subdivision called Morseland Gardens, an enterprise of the Winter Park Land Company.

The following comments are based on an analysis made by Robert F. Wilkinson (President 1980-1981) made in April 1981.

1. The Deed for the purchase of lots 32, 33, 48 and 49 was recorded on June 2, 1945. Annex A lists the restrictions contained in the Deed and an interpretation of their status.
2. A release for the erection of the Clubhouse was obtained from the Winter Park Land Co. and Morseland Gardens owners in June 1945.
3. The Deed for the purchase of lots 31 and 47 was obtained June 1952, at which time release of restrictions was also obtained from the Winter Park Land Co. and the Morseland Gardens owners. Restrictions and an interpretation of their status is contained in Annex B.
4. a) Most restrictions concerning property use appear to have lapsed on January 1, 1975, no action to renew them having been taken.

b) The option to repurchase by the Winter Park Land Co. may possibly be still valid although the wording in the two deeds is not identical and is perhaps ambiguous.

c) The Morseland owners may still have some say in subsequent use for other-than-Club purposes.

LOTS 32, 33, 48, 49

1. One private dwelling for one family, private garage and quarters for servant, etc., attached to house.

2. No structure to be erected without approval of plans by Grantor or his architect.

3. No tents or temporary structures without Grantor's approval. No advertising signs.

4. One dwelling per lot.

5. No outbuilding without Grantor's approval.

6. No fences, walls, etc. without Grantor's approval.

7. No horses, cows, hogs, etc.

8. Restrictions may be waived only by Grantor and majority of Morseland Gardens owners.

9. No trees removed without Grantor's consent.

10. Rear five feet of property subject to an easement for utilities.

11. No sale, renting, mortgaging, etc. to Blacks. Not to be occupied by Blacks other than servants.

12. Grantor has the right of injunction to enforce restrictions.

13. Invalidity of one restriction does not affect others.

Note: On granting releases for erection of Clubhouse, Winter Park Land Co. and Morseland Gardens owners stipulated that:

1) Club will not be used for public evening dances.

2) Winter Park Land Co. has option to purchase for $5,000.00 if the Club wishes to dispose of the property.

3) If the Club ceases to occupy the property, then any disposal shall be for purposes not in conflict with City Ordinances and agreed to by three-fourths of Morseland Gardens owners.

LOTS 31 AND 47

1-9. Identical with restrictions on Lots 32, 33, 48 and 49.

10. Utility easement

11. If Club does not use lots for Clubhouse and decides to dispose of them, Grantor may repurchase for *not less than* $5,000.00.

12. No sale, renting, mortgaging, etc. to Blacks. Not to be occupied by Blacks other than servants.

13. Right of injunction to entrance restrictions.

14. Invalidity of one restriction does not affect others.

15. No parking on Lot 47 so long as Campbells own 813 Park Ave. North.

Notes:

1. On granting release for erection of the Clubhouse, Winter Park Land Co. and Morseland Gardens owners stipulated that, if the Club does not utilize the property, the release of restrictions becomes null and void and the property will revert to residential use.

2. Some of the restrictions were nullified by the Civil Rights Act of 1964 and many other restrictions have lapsed with the passage of time.

APPENDIX C

Committees Through the Years

If the Intellectual Activities are the soul of the Club, then the Committees certainly are the muscle. Without them, the management, the investing, the record-keeping, the outreach, the fund-raising, the maintenance, the recruiting and retention, the dining and talent booking—and even the Activities themselves—would not occur.

Whether standing, ad hoc, or sub, the Committees keep the Club organized, functioning, and progressing, supported by or in tandem with the Staff. In 2010, there were more than forty Standing Committees, thirty-one of them headed by a Vice President and twelve reporting directly to the President. These Committees are continuous from year to year. In addition, there were many subcommittees that expire at the end of a fiscal year, plus ad hoc Committees, appointed for a specific task or reason and expiring at the end of the fiscal year.

The first mention of Committees in the Club *Yearbook* was in 1943-44, when four Standing Committees were listed: Program, House, Memorials, and Membership—each one chaired by a Vice President, a custom that has continued through the years.

By 1959, fourteen committees were listed:

Executive (today's Executive Board)	Memorials
Program/Pow Wow	Library
House and Grounds	Cooperation with Negro Residents
Finance	Member Interracial Council
Membership	Student Aid Trustees
Social	Summer Pow Wows
Fellowship	Rollins College Scholarships

A review of past Committees was conducted by Member H. Ellsworth Miller in 1994, and it listed a wide variety of groups over the years. Some highlights:

- Publication and Publicity appeared for the first time in 1960-61.
- A *Yearbook* Committee was not appointed until 1973-74.
- The first mention of a Nominating Committee was in 1975-76, although the Bylaws provided for such a Committee as early as 1938.
- 1976-77 saw a College Committee and a Home Service Referrals Committee, followed the next year by Interiors and Arts as well as an Annual Inventory Committee.
- The Public Address and Projection Committee became separate Committees in 1978-79, and Rogues Gallery was first listed the following year.
- SPARKS (Showcase for Promotion of the Arts and Related Skills) appeared in 1983-84. By the next year, SPARKS had disappeared.
- The Club entered the electronics age in 1989-90, with the appearance of a Computer Committee. Subcommittees that year included Video Selection as well as Background Music.

In 1992-93, the number of Committees had reached forty, and subsequent years indicate that the Committees were moving toward the pattern in place in 2010. Working Committees that year are listed here.

COMMITTEES 2010

Advisory to the President
Council of Presidents Emeriti
Legal
Computer Systems

Reporting to the President
Public Relations
Auditor
Nominating
Parliamentarian
Club Times
Archivist
Human Resource
Club Operating Manual
Library
Office Assistance
Records Management
Preceptor Program and Speaker
  Service

**Reporting to Vice President
Development**
Development
Community Assistance
Education Assistance

**Reporting to the Vice
President Programs**
Programs
Seating
Cashiers/Greeters
After Hours
Catering/Hospitality
Gallery Arts

**Reporting to the Vice
President House and Grounds**
House and Grounds
Plans, Programs, and
  Budgeting
Interior Refurbishment
Landscaping
Audio-Visual
Rental

**Reporting to the Vice
President Finance**
Finance

**Reporting to the Vice
President Membership**
Membership
New Member Orientation
Club Family Album
Memorials
New Members Activity Review
Amigo
Care
Receptions/Special Functions

**Reporting to the Vice
President
Intellectual Activities**
Intellectual Activity Groups
(see Chapter 11)

Reporting to the Secretary
Yearbook

Some Club Committees wax and wane—others are more stable. The demands of some years create opportunities for service and active participation by the members. In true democratic tradition, the Committees provide objective perspectives in Club management. Their diligence is responsible for Club progress. They speak for — and of — the membership. Their contributions have been and are the muscle of the Club.

APPENDIX D

Presidents

In the first seventy-five years of the Club, there were seventy-one elected Presidents. Most served for one year. Five, however, served two consecutive years (George M. Whicher, Clarence M. Day, Lester Schriver, J. Richard Sewell, and Dan Schulz) and two (John Milton Moore and David Stonecliffe) served two nonconsecutive terms.

Three women have been elected to the presidency: M. Elizabeth Brothers (who was also the first woman admitted to the Club, in 1981), Diane Sandquist, and Max Reed. One married couple has served separate terms, Bob and Max Reed.

As of 2010-11, sixteen Past Presidents remained active members of the Club. They are marked with an asterisk in this list.

George M. Whicher	1934-36	John Gowdy	1944-45
Eugene R. Shippen	1936-37	James F. Hosic	1945-46
Edward M. Davis	1937-38	Eugene R. Smith	1946-47
John Milton Moore	1938-39	Russell P. Jameson	1947-48
Arthur M. Harris	1939-40	Oliver K. Eaton	1948-49
George W. Woodbury	1940-41	Betram B. Scott	1949-50
George G. Scott	1941-42	William Trufant Foster	1950
John Milton Moore	1942-43	Clarence M. Day	1950-52
Henry D. Sleeper	1943-44	James C. Moore	1952-53

Adelbert H. Morrison	1953-54	Everett B. Hales	1982-83
William L. Richardson	1954-55	Harold R. Florea	1983-84
Wendell G. Wilcox	1955-56	Robert L. Parry	1984-85
William E. Stark	1956-57	Walter W. Tolson	1985-86
Clinton L. Ruch	1957-58	Harry F. Schroeter	1986-87
Wesley Frost	1958-59	John B. Bond	1987-88
Hallam H. Anderson	1959-60	David W. Stonecliffe	1988-89
Paul L. Thompson	1960-61	John G. Heiland	1989-90
Arthur W. Nelson	1961-62	*Joseph Terranova, Jr	1990-91
Victor R. Gardner	1962-63	J. B. Lea	1991-92
James R. Welsh	1963-64	Erwin A. Britton	1992-93
Walter R. Cremeans	1964-65	Chedo P. Graham	1993-94
Elmer J. Shafer	1965-66	David Stonecliffe	1994-95
Billings M. McArthur	1966-67	*Donald R. Meckstroth	1995-96
Edward L. Troxell	1967-68	*J. Richard Sewell	1996-98
Edgerton B. Williams	1968-69	Richard M. Artz	1998-99
John G. Van Deusen	1969-70	*M. Elizabeth Brothers	1999-00
Lester O. Schriver	1970-72	*William J. Munsie	2000-01
August E. Johansen	1972-73	*Diane L. Sandquist	2001-02
W. Meredith Behrens	1973-74	*George L. Wannall	2002-03
Frank C. Linn	1974-75	*Frederick A. Rosenthal	2003-04
Charles S. Duffy	1975-76	*Dan Schulz	2004-06
Erwin G. Steinwart	1976-77	*Joseph J. Rizzo	2006-07
Ross Pollock	1977-78	*Robert M. Reed	2007-08
Gill W. Buhrmann	1978-79	*Frank Paul Barber	2008-09
William B. Edmands	1979-80	*Maxine K. Reed	2009-10
*Robert F. Wilkinson	1980-81	*Paul Enchelmayer	2010-11
*Virgil L. Hartsock	1981-82		